MINISTRY
TO THE Cities

Prepared by the Ellen G. White® Estate
12501 Old Columbia Pike
Silver Spring, Maryland 20904, U.S.A.

Published by Review and Herald® Publishing Association

At the time Ellen White wrote, mostly in the nineteenth century, "men" and the masculine pronoun "he" were commonly used to include both men and women. This was Ellen White's custom. No doubt if she were writing today, she would use more gender-inclusive language. This is evident by the fact that some file copies of her letters and manuscripts contain the handwritten words "and women" inserted after the word "men."

This book was
Copyedited by James Cavil
Designed by Ron J. Pride
Cover photo © Thinkstock.com
Typeset: Bembo 11.5/14

PRINTED IN U.S.A.

16   15   14   13   12   5   4   3   2   1

Library of Congress Cataloging
White, Ellen Gould Harmon, 1827-1915.
  Ministry to the cities / Ellen G. White.
      p. cm.
  1. City missions. 2. Evangelistic work. 3. Adventists—Doctrines. 4. Seventh-Day Adventists—Doctrines. I. Title.
  BV2653.W44 2012
  253.09173'2—dc23

                                          2012006771

ISBN 978-0-8280-2665-9

Jesse & Lucille Armour
706-393-4323

I started to reading
Sunday, morning Oct.

MINISTRY

have 120 days
to finish it.

TO THE Cities

ELLEN G. WHITE

REVIEW AND HERALD® PUBLISHING ASSOCIATION

Since 1861 | www.reviewandherald.com

ELLEN WHITE'S
EARLIEST APPEAL
for
CITIES AND VILLAGES

The cities and villages constitute a part of [God's] vineyard. These must be worked, and not passed by. Satan will try to interpose himself, so as to discourage the workers, and prevent them from giving the message of light and warning in the more important as well as in the more secluded places. Desperate efforts will be made to turn the people from the truth of God to falsehood. Angels of heaven are commissioned to work with the efforts of God's appointed messengers. The preachers of the truth must encourage faith and hope, as did Christ, your living head. Keep humble and contrite in heart before God. Maintain an unwavering faith in the promises of God.—Manuscript 1, 1874 (similar to *Testimonies for the Church,* vol. 7, pp. 34, 35).

Table of Contents

Foreword..9

Lessons From Scripture Regarding City Evangelism 11

An Essential Work for This Time 25

Challenges of the City...33

Total Involvement Needed 47

A Strategy for Reaching the Cities 55

Nurturing and Training Workers 69

Teaching and Reaping Methods 86

Working Inside and Outside Cities 112

Christ-centered Health Ministry 123

Planting Churches in the Cities.......................................140

The Work in Specific Cities...151

A Case Study...185

Epilogue 195

FOREWORD

Psalm 48 is often viewed as the city dweller's twenty-third psalm. The Lord is "greatly to be praised in the city of our God" (verse 1, NKJV). It is God's presence in the city that makes it beautiful in its loftiness, "the joy of the whole earth, . . . the city of the great King" (verse 2, NKJV). That God could so identify with an earthly city should alert us to see the potential of the cities of today through God's eyes.

Cities, though, have often been arrayed against God. Such cities were dominant when the Bible was written. Jesus, Moses, David, Daniel, and most of the other Bible prophets had to deal with cities, some of which were huge for that day. Nineveh was "an exceedingly great city, a three-day journey in extent" (Jonah 3:3, NKJV), having "more than one hundred and twenty thousand persons" (Jonah 4:11, NKJV). Babylon had about 10 miles (16 kilometers) of walls surrounding a major populace and monumental buildings that included one of the seven wonders of the ancient world. New Testament Ephesus had street lighting along its main artery, the famed Arcadiane. Rome, Alexandria, Antioch, Athens, Corinth, Susa, and Thebes were among the great cities of Bible times.

Paul was Christianity's premier evangelist to the major cities of the Roman Empire. Peter, Philip, Apollos, and other Christian leaders evangelized the cities as well. Those accustomed to thinking of cities as places of evil should remember that in vision John saw God's ultimate intentions for humanity as a city of incomparable glory and joy.

When Jesus walked the earth, He "went about all the cities and villages," teaching, preaching, and healing. The crowds moved Him deeply: "When He saw the multitudes, He was moved with compassion for them, because they were . . . like sheep having no shepherd" (Matthew 9:35, 36, NKJV). Today most of the world's population lives in cities. Does Jesus care for them any less than He did for those in the cities 2,000 years ago? It is no wonder that Ellen G. White was given so much counsel on the city to equip the church for comprehensive urban evangelism and ministry. Yet her instruction on city work is less well known than her appeals for locating in more rural settings. The brief compilation *Country Living* (1946) has brought well-deserved attention to those appeals. As a complement to that collection, the current volume, *Ministry to the Cities,* is designed to help readers understand God's plan for doing ministry in the city. Prepared in the offices of the Ellen G. White Estate, it draws not only from the articles, books, and pamphlets of Ellen G. White, but also from her letters and manuscripts. It is not an exhaustive compilation of her counsel on the cities, but as a representative collection it is highly informative. It covers many areas of instruction Ellen White received for the church and its outreach to the world's cities. To aid the reader, years are given for the statements included in this volume. For letters and manuscripts, the year indicates the time of writing; for other sources, it is the time of first publication in the stated form. Citations to *Testimonies for the Church,* volumes 1-5, reflect the year of their earlier publication as *Testimony* pamphlets.

Many decades have passed since Ellen White wrote the last of her counsels. In some respects the conditions that we face today differ from those she addressed. The reader should remember that time, location, and other factors must be considered in laying plans for today's work. Conditions may change, the methods for dealing with them may vary, but the principles behind the counsels remain the same. These principles should inform and guide our efforts in meeting today's challenges.

As Christ's second coming approaches, Ellen White's words take on new urgency: "The work in the cities is the essential work for this time. When the cities are worked as God would have them, the result will be the setting in operation of a mighty movement such as we have not yet witnessed" (*Medical Ministry,* p. 304). It is our hope and prayer that *Ministry to the Cities* may help readers become more committed to implementing the counsels we have received and more effective in reaching the cities with Christ's last-day message.

—The Trustees of the Ellen G. White Estate
Silver Spring, Maryland

Chapter 1

LESSONS FROM SCRIPTURE REGARDING CITY EVANGELISM

(The Old Testament)

THE ANTEDILUVIAN WORLD—ENOCH

Earliest Example of City Evangelism.—Enoch walked with God, and yet he did not live in . . . any city polluted with . . . violence and wickedness.—Manuscript 94, 1903 (*Evangelism,* p. 78).

Enoch Did Not Live With the Wicked.—He [Enoch] did not make his abode with the wicked. . . . He placed himself and his family where the atmosphere would be as pure as possible. Then at times he went forth to the inhabitants of the world with his God-given message. . . . After proclaiming his message, he always took back with him to his place of retirement some who had received the warning.—Manuscript 42, 1900 (*Maranatha,* p. 184).

Enoch's Methods Will Become Our Methods.—Wise plans are to be laid, in order that . . . work may be done to the best possible advantage. More and more, as wickedness increases in the great cities, we shall have to work them from outpost centers. This is the way Enoch labored in the days before the flood, when wickedness was rife in every populous community, and when violence was in the land.—*Review and Herald,* September 27, 1906.

SODOM

Love for Souls Motivated Abraham's Prayer.—Though

Lot had become a dweller in Sodom, he did not partake in the iniquity of its inhabitants. Abraham thought that in that populous city there must be other worshipers of the true God. And in view of this he pleaded, "That be far from Thee to do after this manner, to slay the righteous with the wicked: . . . that be far from Thee: Shall not the Judge of all the earth do right?" Abraham asked not once merely, but many times. Waxing bolder as his requests were granted, he continued until he gained the assurance that if even ten righteous persons could be found in it, the city would be spared.

Love for perishing souls inspired Abraham's prayer. While he loathed the sins of that corrupt city, he desired that the sinners might be saved. His deep interest for Sodom shows the anxiety that we should feel for the impenitent. We should cherish hatred of sin, but pity and love for the sinner. All around us are souls going down to ruin as hopeless, as terrible, as that which befell Sodom. Every day the probation of some is closing. Every hour some are passing beyond the reach of mercy. And where are the voices of warning and entreaty to bid the sinner flee from this fearful doom? Where are the hands stretched out to draw him back from death? Where are those who with humility and persevering faith are pleading with God for him?—*Patriarchs and Prophets,* pp. 139, 140. (1890)

Christians Can Greatly Impact Cities.—If God would have saved Sodom for the sake of ten righteous persons, what would be the influence for good that might go out as the result of the faithfulness of the people of God if every one who professed the name of Christ were also clothed with His righteousness?—*Signs of the Times,* May 2, 1895 (*In Heavenly Places,* p. 104).

NINEVEH

Many Will Respond to God's Call.—Nineveh, wicked though it had become, was not wholly given over to evil. He who "beholdeth all the sons of men" (Psalm 33:13) and "seeth every previous thing" (Job 28:10) perceived in that city many who were reaching

• out after something better and higher, and who, if granted opportunity to learn of the living God, would put away their evil deeds and worship Him. And so in His wisdom God revealed Himself to them in an unmistakable manner, to lead them, if possible, to repentance.

The instrument chosen for this work was the prophet Jonah, the son of Amittai. To him came the word of the Lord, "Arise, go to Nineveh, that great city, and cry against it; for their wickedness is come up before me" (Jonah 1:1, 2). . . .

As Jonah entered the city, he began at once to "cry against" it the message, "Yet forty days, and Nineveh shall be overthrown" (Jonah 3:4). From street to street he went, sounding the note of warning.

The message was not in vain. The cry that rang through the streets of the godless city was passed from lip to lip until all the inhabitants had heard the startling announcement. The Spirit of God pressed the message home to every heart and caused multitudes to tremble because of their sins and to repent in deep humiliation.—*Prophets and Kings,* pp. 265-270. (1917)

JERUSALEM—KING JOSIAH'S REVIVAL

Impact of Leaders Not to Be Underestimated.—The king [Josiah] must leave with God the events of the future; he could not alter the eternal decrees of Jehovah. But in announcing the retributive judgments of Heaven, the Lord had not withdrawn opportunity for repentance and reformation; and Josiah, discerning in this a willingness on the part of God to temper His judgments with mercy, determined to do all in his power to bring about decided reforms. He arranged at once for a great convocation, to which were invited the elders and magistrates in Jerusalem and Judah, together with the common people. These, with the priests and Levites, met the king in the court of the temple.

To this vast assembly the king himself read "all the words of the book of the covenant which was found in the house of the Lord" (2 Kings 23:2). The royal reader was deeply affected, and he delivered his message with the pathos of a broken heart. His hearers were profoundly moved. The intensity of feeling revealed in the countenance of the king, the solemnity of the message itself, the warning of judgments impending—all these had their effect, and many determined to join with the king in seeking forgiveness.

Josiah now proposed that those highest in authority unite with the people in solemnly covenanting before God to cooperate with one another in an effort to institute decided changes. "The king stood by a pillar, and made a covenant before the Lord, to walk after the Lord, and to keep His commandments and His testimonies and His statutes with all their heart and all their soul, to perform the words of this covenant that were written in this book." The response was more hearty than the king had dared hope for: "All the people stood to the covenant" (verse 3).

In the reformation that followed, the king turned his attention to the destruction of every vestige of idolatry. . . . So long had the inhabitants of the land followed . . . the surrounding nations in bowing down to images of wood and stone, that it seemed almost beyond the power of man to remove every trace of these evils. But Josiah persevered in his effort to cleanse the land. Sternly he met idolatry by slaying "all the priests of the high places"; "moreover the workers with familiar spirits, and the wizards, and the images, and the idols, and all the abominations that were spied in the land of Judah and in Jerusalem, did Josiah put away, that he might perform the words of the law which were written in the book that Hilkiah the priest found in the house of the Lord" (verses 20, 24).—*Prophets and Kings,* pp. 400, 401. (1917)

(The New Testament)

CHRIST'S MISSION CHARTER

Go to the People.—The gospel commission is the great missionary charter of Christ's kingdom. The disciples were to work earnestly for souls, giving to all the invitation of mercy. They were not to wait for the people to come to them; they were to go to the people with their message.—*The Acts of the Apostles,* p. 28. (1911)

Christ's Earthly Ministry Illustrated the Gospel Commission.—He who is the light and life of the gospel was made flesh and dwelt among us. A sympathizer with humanity, He fed the hungry, healed the sick, and went about through all the cities of the land doing good to men. All our works are to be wrought in Christ. By becoming partakers of His nature, His followers are to work His works. The ministry of Christ for men was the interpretation of His great commission to the disciples, "Go ye into all the world, and preach the gospel to every creature."— Manuscript 1, 1908 (*Manuscript Releases,* vol. 5, pp. 213, 214).

JESUS, THE MASTER TEACHER

Jesus Taught by Example.—It was by personal contact and association that Jesus trained His disciples. Sometimes He taught them, sitting among them on the mountainside; sometimes beside the sea, or walking with them by the way, He revealed the mysteries of the kingdom of God. He did not sermonize as men do today. Wherever hearts were open to receive the divine message, He unfolded the truths of the way of salvation. He did not command His disciples to do this or that, but said, "Follow Me." On His journeys through country and cities He took them with Him, that they might see how He taught the people. He linked their interest with His, and they united with Him in the work.—*The Desire of Ages,* p. 152. (1898)

Jesus Mingled With Those He Served.—During His earthly ministry Christ began to break down the partition wall between Jew and Gentile, and to preach salvation to all mankind. Though He was a Jew, He mingled freely with the Samaritans, setting at nought the Pharisaic customs of the Jews with regard to this despised people. He slept under their roofs, ate at their tables, and taught in their streets.—*The Acts of the Apostles,* p. 19. (1911)

Jesus Chose Capernaum for Its Evangelistic Potential.—During His earthly ministry the Saviour took advantage of the opportunities to be found along the great thoroughfares of travel. It was at Capernaum that Jesus dwelt at the intervals of His journeys to and fro, and it came to be known as "His own city." This city was well adapted to be the center of the Saviour's work. Being on the highway from Damascus to Jerusalem and Egypt, and to the Mediterranean Sea, it was a great thoroughfare of travel. People from many lands passed through the city or tarried for rest on their journeyings to and fro. Here Jesus could meet all nations and all ranks, the rich and great, as well as the poor and lowly; and His lessons would be carried to other countries and into many households. Investigation of the prophecies would thus be excited; attention would be directed to the Saviour, and His mission would be brought before the world.—*Testimonies for the Church,* vol. 9, p. 121. (1909)

New Testament Cities

JERUSALEM

Gospel to Be Proclaimed in all Circumstances.—Christ told His disciples that they were to begin their work at Jerusalem. That city had been the scene of His amazing sacrifice for the human race. There, clad in the garb of humanity, He had walked and talked with men, and few had discerned how near heaven came to earth. There He had been condemned and crucified. In Jerusalem were many who secretly believed Jesus of Nazareth to be the Messiah, and many who had been deceived by priests and rulers. To these the gospel must be proclaimed. They were to be called to repentance. The wonderful truth that through Christ alone could remission of sins be obtained was to be made plain. And it was while all Jerusalem was stirred by the thrilling events of the past few weeks, that the preaching of the disciples would make the deepest impression.—*The Acts of the Apostles,* pp. 31, 32. (1911)

Disciples Credited Others for Souls Converted.—In Jerusalem, the stronghold of Judaism, thousands openly declared their faith in Jesus of Nazareth as the Messiah.

The disciples were astonished and overjoyed at the greatness of the harvest of souls. They did not regard this wonderful ingathering as the result of their own efforts; they realized that they were entering into other men's labors.—*The Acts of the Apostles,* p. 44. (1911)

ANTIOCH OF SYRIA

Name "Christian" Resulted From Christ-centered City Witness.—In the populous city of Antioch, [the apostle] Paul found an excellent field of labor. His learning, wisdom, and zeal exerted a powerful influence over the inhabitants and frequenters of that city of culture; and he proved just the help that Barnabas needed. For a year the two disciples labored unitedly in faithful ministry, bringing to many a saving knowledge of Jesus of Nazareth, the world's Redeemer.

It was in Antioch that the disciples were first called Christians. The name was given them because Christ was the main theme of their preaching, their teaching, and their conversation.—*The Acts of the Apostles,* pp. 156, 157. (1911)

City Church Members to Join Others in Service.—The example of the followers of Christ at Antioch should be an inspiration to every believer living in the great cities of the world today. While it is in the order of God that chosen workers of consecration and talent should be stationed in important centers of population to lead out in public efforts, it is also His purpose that the church members living in these cities shall use their God-given talents in working for souls. There are rich blessings in store for those who surrender fully to the call of God. As such workers endeavor to win souls to Jesus, they will find that many who never could have been reached in any other way are ready to respond to intelligent personal effort.

The cause of God in the earth today is in need of living representatives of Bible truth. The ordained ministers alone are not equal to the task of warning the great cities. God is calling not only upon ministers, but also upon physicians, nurses, colporteurs, Bible workers, and other consecrated laymen of varied talent who have a knowledge of the word of God and who know the power of His grace, to consider the needs of the unwarned cities. Time is rapidly passing, and there is much to be done. Every agency must be set in operation, that present opportunities may be wisely improved.— *The Acts of the Apostles,* pp. 158, 159. (1911)

CHURCHES ORGANIZED
IN CITIES OF CENTRAL ASIA MINOR

Establishment of Churches Stabilizes New Members.— The day following the stoning of Paul, the apostles departed for Derbe, where their labors were blessed, and many souls were led to receive Christ as the Saviour. But "when they had preached the gospel to that city, and had taught many," neither Paul nor Barnabas was content to take up work elsewhere without confirming the faith of the converts whom they had been compelled to leave alone for a time in the places where they had recently labored. And so, undaunted by danger, "they returned again to Lystra, and to Iconium, and Antioch, confirming the souls of the disciples, and exhorting them to continue in the faith." Many had accepted the glad tidings of the gospel and had thus exposed themselves to reproach and opposition. These the apostles sought to establish in the faith in order that the work done might abide.

As an important factor in the spiritual growth of the new converts the apostles were careful to surround them with the safeguards of gospel order. Churches were duly organized in all places in Lycaonia and Pisidia where there were believers. Officers were appointed in each church, and proper order and system were established for the conduct of all the affairs pertaining to the spiritual welfare of the believers.—*The Acts of the Apostles*, p. 185. (1911)

THESSALONICA

Paul Taught Scripture-based Truths.—As with holy boldness Paul proclaimed the gospel in the synagogue at Thessalonica, a flood of light was thrown upon the true meaning of the rites and ceremonies connected with the tabernacle service. He carried the minds of his hearers beyond the earthly service and the ministry of Christ in the heavenly sanctuary, to the time when, having completed His mediatorial work, Christ would come again in power and great glory, and establish His kingdom on the earth. Paul was a believer in the second coming of Christ; so clearly and forcibly did he present the truths concerning this event, that upon the minds of many who heard there was made an impression which never wore away.

For three successive Sabbaths Paul preached to the Thessalonians, reasoning with them from the Scriptures regarding the life, death, resurrection, office work, and future glory of Christ, the "Lamb slain from the foundation of the world" (Revelation 13:8). He exalted Christ, the proper understanding of whose ministry is the key that unlocks the Old Testament Scriptures, giving access to their rich treasures.

As the truths of the gospel were thus proclaimed in Thessalonica with mighty power, the attention of large congregations was arrested. "Some of them believed, and consorted with Paul and Silas; and of the devout Greeks a great multitude, and of the chief women not a few."—*The Acts of the Apostles*, pp. 228, 229. (1911)

ATHENS

Unchurched Not to Be Overlooked.—While waiting for Silas and Timothy, Paul was not idle. He "disputed . . . in the synagogue with the Jews, and with the devout persons, and in the market daily with them that met with him." But his principal work in Athens was to bear the tidings of salvation to those who had no intelligent conception of God and of His purpose in behalf of the fallen race. The apostle was soon to meet paganism in its most subtle, alluring form.—*The Acts of the Apostles,* pp. 234, 235. (1911)

Evangelize the Wise and Educated.—They [the local leading philosophers] . . . conducted him [Paul] to Mars' Hill. This was one of the most sacred spots in all Athens, and its recollections and associations were such as to cause it to be regarded with a superstitious reverence that in the minds of some amounted to dread. It was in this place that matters connected with religion were often carefully considered by men who acted as final judges on all the more important moral as well as civil questions.

Here, away from the noise and bustle of crowded thoroughfares, and the tumult of promiscuous* discussion, the apostle could be heard without interruption. Around him gathered poets, artists, and philosophers—the scholars and sages of Athens, who thus addressed him: "May we know what this new doctrine, whereof thou speakest, is? for thou bringest certain strange things to our ears: we would know therefore what these things mean."—*The Acts of the Apostles,* p. 236. (1911)

Local Culture Impacted Paul's Message.—With hand outstretched toward the temple crowded with idols, Paul poured out the burden of his soul, and exposed the fallacies of the religion of the Athenians. The wisest of his hearers were astonished as they listened to his reasoning. He showed himself familiar with their works of art, their literature, and their religion. Pointing to their statuary and idols, he declared that God could not be likened to forms of man's devising. These graven images could not, in the faintest sense, represent the glory of Jehovah. He reminded them that these images had no life, but were controlled by human power, moving only when the hands of men moved them; and therefore those who worshiped

---

* Nineteenth-century definition: without organization or purpose; varied, mixed.

them were in every way superior to that which they worshiped.

Paul drew the minds of his idolatrous hearers beyond the limits of their false religion to a true view of the Deity, whom they had styled the "Unknown God."—*The Acts of the Apostles,* p. 237. (1911)

CORINTH

Change Methods if Results Are Small.—During the first century of the Christian Era, Corinth was one of the leading cities, not only of Greece, but of the world. Greeks, Jews, and Romans, with travelers from every land, thronged its streets, eagerly intent on business and pleasure. A great commercial center, situated within easy access of all parts of the Roman Empire, it was an important place in which to establish memorials for God and His truth.

Among the Jews who had taken up their residence in Corinth were Aquila and Priscilla, who afterward became distinguished as earnest workers for Christ. Becoming acquainted with the character of these persons, Paul "abode with them."

At the very beginning of his labors in this thoroughfare of travel, Paul saw on every hand serious obstacles to the progress of his work. The city was almost wholly given up to idolatry. Venus was the favorite goddess, and with the worship of Venus were connected many demoralizing rites and ceremonies. The Corinthians had become conspicuous, even among the heathen, for their gross immorality. They seemed to have little thought or care beyond the pleasures and gaieties of the hour.

In preaching the gospel in Corinth, the apostle followed a course different from that which had marked his labors at Athens. While in the latter place, he had sought to adapt his style to the character of his audience; he had met logic with logic, science with science, philosophy with philosophy. As he thought of the time thus spent, and realized that his teaching in Athens had been productive of but little fruit, he decided to follow another plan of labor in Corinth in his efforts to arrest the attention of the careless and the indifferent. He determined to avoid elaborate arguments and discussions, and "not to know anything" among the Corinthians "save Jesus Christ, and Him crucified." He would preach to them "not with enticing words of man's wisdom, but in demonstration of the Spirit and of power" (1 Corinthians 2:2, 4).

Jesus, whom Paul was about to present before the Greeks in Corinth as the Christ, was a Jew of lowly origin, reared in a town proverbial for its wickedness. He had been rejected by His own nation and at last crucified as a malefactor. The Greeks believed that there was need of elevating the human race, but they regarded the study of philosophy and science as the only means of attaining to true elevation and honor. Could Paul lead them to believe that faith in the power of this obscure Jew would uplift and ennoble every power of the being?

To the minds of multitudes living at the present time, the cross of Calvary is surrounded by sacred memories. Hallowed associations are connected with the scenes of the crucifixion. But in Paul's day the cross was regarded with feelings of repulsion and horror. To uphold as the Saviour of mankind one who had met death on the cross would naturally call forth ridicule and opposition.

Paul well knew how his message would be regarded by both the Jews and the Greeks of Corinth. "We preach Christ crucified," he admitted, "unto the Jews a stumbling block, and unto the Greeks foolishness" (1 Corinthians 1:23). Among his Jewish hearers there were many who would be angered by the message he was about to proclaim. In the estimation of the Greeks his words would be absurd folly. He would be looked upon as weak-minded for attempting to show how the cross could have any connection with the elevation of the race or the salvation of mankind.—*The Acts of the Apostles,* pp. 243-245. (1911)

Human to Be Hidden Behind the Divine.—The apostle's [Paul's] efforts were not confined to public speaking; there were many who could not have been reached in that way. He spent much time in house-to-house labor, thus availing himself of the familiar intercourse*

---

* Nineteenth-century definition: communication, interaction.

of the home circle. He visited the sick and the sorrowing, comforted the afflicted, and lifted up the oppressed. And in all that he said and did he magnified the name of Jesus. Thus he labored, "in weakness, and in fear, and in much trembling" (1 Corinthians 2:3). He trembled lest his teaching should reveal the impress of the human rather than the divine.—*The Acts of the Apostles,* p. 250. (1911)

Lowliest Can Become Monuments to God's Greatness.—Paul's efforts in Corinth were not without fruit. Many turned from the worship of idols to serve the living God, and a large church was enrolled under the banner of Christ. Some were rescued from among the most dissipated of the Gentiles and became monuments of the mercy of God and the efficacy of the blood of Christ to cleanse from sin.—*The Acts of the Apostles,* p. 252. (1911)

EPHESUS

If Opposition Becomes Strong, Change Location.—As was his custom, Paul had begun his work at Ephesus by preaching in the synagogue of the Jews. He continued to labor there for three months, "disputing and persuading the things concerning the kingdom of God." At first he met with a favorable reception; but as in other fields, he was soon violently opposed. "Divers were hardened, and believed not, but spake evil of that way before the multitude." As they persisted in their rejection of the gospel, the apostle ceased to preach in the synagogue.

The Spirit of God had wrought with and through Paul in his labors for his countrymen. Sufficient evidence had been presented to convince all who honestly desired to know the truth.—*The Acts of the Apostles,* p. 285. (1911)

ROME

Existing Churches to Plant New Churches.—To see the Christian faith firmly established at the great center of the known world was one of his [Paul's] dearest hopes and most cherished plans. A church had already been raised up at Rome, and the apostle desired to secure their cooperation in the work which he hoped to accomplish. To prepare the way for his labors among these brethren, as yet strangers, he addressed them by letter, announcing his purpose to visit Rome, and also by their aid to plant the standard of the cross in Spain.—*Sketches From the Life of Paul,* p. 187. (1883)

Paul the Prisoner Still Witnessed.—Rome was at this time the metropolis of the world. The haughty Caesars were giving laws to nearly every nation upon the earth. King and courtier were either ignorant of the humble Nazarene or regarded Him with hatred and derision. And yet in less than two years the gospel found its way from the prisoner's lowly home into the imperial halls. Paul is in bonds as an evildoer; but "the word of God is not bound" (2 Timothy 2:9).—*The Acts of the Apostles,* pp. 461, 462. (1911)

Public Officials Can Enhance Evangelistic Possibilities.—Through the favor of those who had Paul in charge, he was permitted to dwell in a commodious house, where he could meet freely with his friends and also present the truth daily to those who came to hear. Thus for two years he continued his labors, "preaching the kingdom of God, and teaching those things which concern the Lord Jesus Christ, with all confidence, no man forbidding him."—*The Acts of the Apostles,* p. 453. (1911)

Converts in Responsible Positions Can Witness Where They Are.—Not only were converts won to the truth in Caesar's household, but after their conversion they remained in that household. They did not feel at liberty to abandon their post of duty because their surroundings were no longer congenial. The truth had found them there, and there they remained, by their changed life and character testifying to the transforming power of the new faith.—*The Acts of the Apostles,* p. 466. (1911)

Chapter 2

AN ESSENTIAL WORK
FOR THIS TIME

God's Perspective to Become Our Perspective.—Oh, that we might see the needs of these cities as God sees them! At such a time as this every hand is to be employed. The Lord is coming; the end is near, yea, it hasteth greatly! In a little while we shall be unable to work with the freedom that we now enjoy. Terrible scenes are before us, and what we do we must do quickly.—*Testimonies for the Church,* vol. 9, p. 101. (1909)

Many Carry No Burden for Souls.—The large cities should have been worked just as soon as the churches received the light, but many have carried no burden for souls, and Satan, finding them susceptible to his temptations, has spoiled their experience. God asks His people to repent, be converted, and to return to their first love, which they have lost by their failure to follow in the footsteps of the self-sacrificing Redeemer.—*Testimonies for the Church,* vol. 9, p. 140. (1909)

Too Little Attention Given to Cities.—Behold the cities, and their need of the gospel! The need of earnest laborers among the multitudes of the cities has been kept before me for more than twenty years. Who are carrying a burden for the large cities? A few have felt the burden, but in comparison with the great need and the many opportunities but little attention has been given to this work.—*Testimonies for the Church,* vol. 9, pp. 97, 98. (1909)

Work for Cities Far Behind God's Plan.—The importance of making our way in the great cities is still kept before me. For many years the Lord has been urging upon us this duty, and yet we see but comparatively little accomplished in our great centers of population. If we do not take up this work in a determined manner, Satan will multiply difficulties which will not be easy to surmount. We are far behind in doing the work that should have been done in these long-neglected cities. The work will now be more difficult than it would have been a few years ago. But if we take up the work in the name of the Lord, barriers will be broken down, and decided victories will be ours.—Letter 148, 1909 (*Medical Ministry,* pp. 301, 302).

Earnest Prayer and Effort Needed for Cities.—We carry too light a burden in behalf of souls unsaved. There never was a time when the world needed us more than it needs us now. All about us are cities unwarned. Souls are perishing, and what are we doing? We need to have a burden for these souls, such as many of us have never experienced. . . .

We do not half believe these truths. If we did, there would be seen more praying and more diligence in trying to carry these truths to the inhabitants of the cities of our land. God is now calling upon us to open up a strong work in the cities.—Manuscript 23, 1910.

Cities to Be Worked Without Delay.—The message that I am bidden to bear to our people at this time is, Work the cities without delay, for time is short. The Lord has kept this work before us for the last twenty years or more. A little has been done in a few places, but much more might be done. I am carrying a burden day and night, because so little is being accomplished to warn the inhabitants of our great centers of population of the judgments that will fall upon the transgressors of God's law.—Letter 168, 1909 (*Medical Ministry,* p. 300).

Message to Be Given Quickly.—The Lord has shown me that there is a work to be done in the cities that is scarcely entered upon. This question of the work in the cities is to become a living question with us. We must not now lay plans for a long, extended work. The message is to be carried quickly. The long delay in carrying out the instruction of the Lord regarding work in the cities has made the work of reaching all classes more difficult. The work must be undertaken at once, and the Lord calls for consecrated laborers who will engage in earnest effort according to the light He has given.—Letter 42, 1909 (*Manuscript Releases,* vol. 17, p. 37).

Workers Needed Everywhere.—Wherever the people of God are placed, in the crowded cities, in the villages, or among the country byways, there is a home mission field, for which a responsibility is laid upon them by their Lord's commission. In every city or settlement where Christians meet to worship God, there are men and women and children to be gathered into the fold. Many have never heard a discourse on God's Word.—Manuscript 87, 1907 (*Manuscript Releases,* vol. 6, p. 323).

Salvation to Be Offered City Inhabitants.—I feel the deepest anxiety as I consider the cities that are yet unworked. Day and night the burden is upon me—the cities must be worked without delay. The message of present truth must be carried to those who have not heard it. . . .

This salvation is for the inhabitants of the unworked cities. Time is rapidly passing into eternity, and these cities have as yet scarcely been touched. There is a power that the Spirit of God can impart to truth. As light is flashed into the mind, a conviction will take hold of hearts that will be too powerful to resist.—Letter 150, 1909.

Message to Convict Hearers.—In our large cities the message is to go forth as a lamp that burneth. God will raise up laborers for this work, and His angels will go before them. Let no one hinder these men of God's appointment. Forbid them not. God has given them their work. Let the message be given with so much power that the hearers shall be convinced.—*Review and Herald,* September 30, 1902 (*Evangelism,* p. 70).

Satan Pleased That Thousands Still in Darkness.— Thousands of people in our cities are left in darkness, and Satan is well pleased with the delay; for this delay gives him opportunity to work in these fields with men of influence to further his plans. Can we now depend upon our men in positions of responsibility to act humbly and nobly their part? Let the watchmen arouse. Let no one continue to be indifferent to the situation. There should be a thorough awakening among the brethren and sisters in all our churches.—Manuscript 21, 1910 (*Medical Ministry,* p. 302).

City Evangelism's Mighty Results Not Yet Witnessed.— There is no change in the messages that God has sent in the past. The work in the cities is the essential work for this time. When the cities are worked as God would have them, the result will be the setting in operation of a mighty movement such as we have not yet witnessed. . . .

As a people we are not half awake to a sense of our necessities and to the times in which we live. Wake up the watchmen. Our first work should be to search our hearts and to become reconverted. We have no time to lose upon unimportant issues.—Letter 46, 1910 (*Medical Ministry,* p. 304).

COWORKERS WITH CHRIST IN THE CITIES

Privileged to Be Coworkers With Christ.—The work of imparting that which he has received will constitute every member of the church a laborer together with God. Of yourself you can do nothing; but Christ is the great worker. It is the privilege of every human being who receives Christ to be a worker together with Him.—*Testimonies for the Church,* vol. 6, p. 449. (1900)

Called to Work in Harmony With Christ.—"As Thou hast

sent Me into the world, even so have I also sent them into the world." It is not for the professing believer to sit down and take life easily, as though there were nothing to be done. There is a great work to be accomplished, and everyone who attains unto eternal life is to cooperate with Jesus Christ. "Neither pray I for these alone," the Saviour said, "but for them also which shall believe on Me through their word; that they all may be one, as Thou, Father, art in Me, and I in Thee, that they also may be one in Us: that the world may believe that Thou hast sent Me. And the glory which Thou gavest Me I have given them; that they may be one, even as We are one: I in them, and Thou in Me, that they may be made perfect in one; and that the world may know that Thou hast sent Me, and hast loved them, as Thou hast loved Me."

Ministers and people are included in these words. All are to be one, even as Christ was one with the Father. There can be no perfection in division. Those who believe in Jesus Christ will be one in their interest for the souls who are perishing out of Christ. The fact is that we have lost sight of our individual responsibility, and we need to take it up in the name of the Lord. When this prayer of Christ's is answered for His people in this age, when this unity exists among Seventh-day Adventists, there will be a tremendous influence going forth from them to the world. Reformations will take place; first in our own ranks, and then in those for whom we labor, will be seen the transformation of character for which Christ so earnestly prayed. . . .

My brethren and sisters, let us study to know what is the work devolving upon us individually. You have something to do for those who are around you, and for those afar off. We have no right to devote all our means for the enjoyment of our present life. We have no right to spend dollars to glorify and indulge self. The judgments of God that are coming upon the earth are certainly not far off, and we should be up and doing our part. As we consider what Christ has suffered for us, we should seek to come into a position of self-denial and self-sacrifice, that we may help in the salvation of the souls that are in peril of everlasting destruction. We can have no excuse to offer to God for neglect of this work.

Are we getting ready for the judgment? Are we preparing to meet the Lord? There is a work to be done for those who are afar off and for those who are nigh. We are to enter cities and towns and villages that have been left without the message of warning for these last days. We do not realize how near we are to the end of this earth's history. We do not realize the value of the souls for whom Christ gave His precious life. We need to put on the robe of Christ's righteousness and work in harmony with Him, in harmony with His ministers, in harmony with all who truly believe the truth for this time.—Manuscript 91, 1909.

Partners With God in Saving Humanity.—It is the grace of God which leads us to obey the law of God, the transcript of the divine character. It is a knowledge of Christ Jesus which we should cultivate to the uttermost of our power in order that we may be doers of His word. . . . Will we make Jesus glad? Will we cause rejoicing among the angels of God? We can do so by cooperating with God in seeking and saving that which was lost. . . . Shall we not cooperate with heavenly angels in the work of saving fallen humanity?—*Sabbath School Worker,* January 1896.

WORKERS TO BE ENCOURAGED

City Workers Need Encouragement.—Those who are engaged in the difficult and trying work in the cities should receive every encouragement possible. Let them not be subjected to unkind criticism from their brethren. We must have a care for the Lord's workers who are opening the light of truth to those who are in the darkness of error. We have a high standard presented before us.—Letter 168, 1909 (*Medical Ministry,* pp. 309, 310).

Not to Become Discouraged.—God's messengers in the great cities are not to become discouraged over the wickedness, the injustice, the depravity, which they are called upon to face while endeavoring to proclaim the glad tidings of salvation. The Lord would cheer every such worker with the same message that He gave to the apostle Paul in wicked Corinth: "Be not afraid, but speak, and hold not thy peace: for I am with thee, and no man shall set on thee to hurt thee: for I have much people in this city" (Acts 18:9, 10). Let those engaged in soul-saving ministry remember that while there are many who will not heed the counsel of God in His word, the whole world will not turn from light and truth, from the invitations of a patient, forbearing Saviour. In every city, filled though it may be with violence and crime, there are many who with proper teaching may learn to become followers of Jesus. Thousands may thus be reached with saving truth and be led to receive Christ as a personal Saviour.—*Prophets and Kings,* p. 277. (1917)

Not to Undo Work God Calls Others to Do.—We should educate ourselves after the divine order, that we may not tear down but build up the interests of humanity. The workers must not draw apart. They will have to meet discouragements from without, and not one who claims to be making up the breach in the law of God, of building up the old waste places, restoring the foundations of many generations, should be found undoing the work that God has set His workmen to accomplish in different branches of His cause.—*Signs of the Times,* July 3, 1893.

Beware of Those Who Try to Discourage City Evangelism.—Our sinful condition of lukewarmness has been coming on for years. We are far behind in following the instructions given to enter the cities, and erect memorials for the cause of present truth. For many years the instruction has been repeated to us regarding the work to be done in the cities; yet there seems to be a deathlike slumber upon many ministers and people. There are a few who have been doing all in their power, but the burden of this work has not been borne upon the hearts of our people; they are not urged to cooperate, and to set in order the things that remain, that are ready to die. . . .

There are some who have not accepted the messages God has

sent, and these have sown the seeds of unbelief until tares have sprung up and multiplied.... Those who have stood directly in the way of the work of God for the past fifteen years are not to be sustained or given influence.—*Review and Herald,* July 23, 1908.

Lack of Encouragement and Support Displeases God.—Let us thank the Lord that there are a few laborers doing everything possible to raise up some memorials for God in our neglected cities. Let us remember that it is our duty to give these workers encouragement. God is displeased with the lack of appreciation and support shown our faithful workers in our large cities.—Manuscript 154, 1902 (*Evangelism,* p. 42).

Satan Tries to Discourage City Workers.—As you look upon the cities, so full of iniquity, Satan will tell you that it is impossible to do them any good. The cities are sadly neglected. You will never know the value of the pearl until you seek earnestly to find it.—Manuscript 13, 1895 (*Manuscript Releases,* vol. 10, p. 227).

Chapter 3

CHALLENGES OF THE CITY

Satan's Work Readily Evident in Cities.—Satan is busily at work in our crowded cities. His work is to be seen in the confusion, the strife and discord between labor and capital, and the hypocrisy that has come into the churches. That men may not take time to meditate, Satan leads them into a round of gaiety* and pleasure-seeking, of eating and drinking. He fills them with ambition to make an exhibition that will exalt self. Step by step, the world is reaching the conditions that existed in the days of Noah. Every conceivable crime is committed. The lust of the flesh, the pride of the eyes, the display of selfishness, the misuse of power, the cruelty, and the force used to cause men to unite with confederacies and unions—binding themselves up in bundles for the burning of the great fires of the last days—all these are the working of Satanic agencies. This round of crime and folly men call "life." . . .

The world, who act as though there were no God, absorbed in selfish pursuits, will soon experience sudden destruction, and shall not escape. Many continue in the careless gratification of self until they become so disgusted with life that they kill themselves. Dancing and carousing, drinking and smoking, indulging their animal passions, they go as an ox to the slaughter. Satan is working with all his art and enchantments to keep men marching blindly onward until the Lord arises out of His place to punish the inhabitants of earth for their iniquities, when the earth shall disclose her blood and no more cover her slain. The whole world appears to be in the march to death.—Manuscript 139, 1903 (*Evangelism*, p. 26).

---

* Nineteenth-century definition: merrymaking, festivity.

33

Satanic Agencies Organize Opposition to God's Law.— Men have confederated to oppose the Lord of hosts. These confederacies will continue until Christ shall leave His place of intercession before the mercy seat and shall put on the garments of vengeance. Satanic agencies are in every city, busily organizing into parties those opposed to the law of God. Professed saints and avowed unbelievers take their stand with these parties. This is no time for the people of God to be weaklings. We cannot afford to be off our guard for one moment.—*Testimonies for the Church,* vol. 8, p. 42. (1904)

Conflict Between Good and Evil Will Last as Long as Time Lasts.—Terrible is the struggle that takes place between the forces of good and of evil in important centers where the messengers of truth are called upon to labor. "We wrestle not against flesh and blood," declares Paul, "but against principalities, against powers, against the rulers of the darkness of this world" (Ephesians 6:12). Till the close of time there will be a conflict between the church of God and those who are under the control of evil angels.—*The Acts of the Apostles,* p. 219. (1911)

Satanic Agencies Increase Difficulty of Working the Cities.—We do not realize the extent to which satanic agencies are at work in these large cities. The work of bringing the message of present truth before the people is becoming more and more difficult. It is essential that new and varied talents unite in intelligent labor for the people.—Letter 168, 1909 (*Medical Ministry,* p. 300).

POVERTY AND UNEMPLOYMENT

People Created for Heaven's Atmosphere.—Men were not created to be subject to poverty, disease, and suffering, not for thoughtless inattention to their physical and spiritual wants, but for dignity, purity, and elevation of character in this life, and for joy unspeakable and full of glory in the future immortal life. The mercies of God are distributed and diversified throughout the earth; and if man would be obedient to nature's laws there would not be a tithe of the misery which now exists. Health and life are imperiled by the indulgence of appetite. Our woes more frequently spring from the improvident use of the abundance than from scarcity. Young men in our cities and towns are surrounded with temptations to indulge in perverted appetite. Vice is gilded over; like apples of Sodom, it appears beautiful without, but is ashes within.—*Forest Park Reporter,* March 30, 1879.

Plight of Poor Requires Urgent Assistance.—In the great cities are multitudes who receive less care and consideration than are given to dumb animals. Think of the families herded together in miserable tenements, many of them dark basements, reeking with dampness and filth. In these wretched places children are born and grow up and die. They see nothing of the beauty of natural things that God has created to delight the senses and uplift the soul. Ragged and half-starved, they live amid vice and depravity, molded in character by the wretchedness and sin that surround them. Children hear the name of God only in profanity. Foul speech, imprecations, and revilings fill their ears. The fumes of liquor and tobacco, sickening stenches, moral degradation, pervert their senses. Thus multitudes are trained to become criminals, foes to society that has abandoned them to misery and degradation.

Not all the poor in the city slums are of this class. God-fearing men and women have been brought to the depths of poverty by illness or misfortune, often through the dishonest scheming of those who live by preying upon their fellows. Many who are upright and well-meaning become poor through lack of industrial training. Through ignorance they are unfitted to wrestle with the difficulties of life. Drifting into the cities, they are often unable to find employment. Surrounded by the sights and sounds of vice, they are subjected to terrible temptation. Herded and often classed with the vicious and degraded, it is only by a superhuman struggle, a more than finite power, that they can be preserved from sinking to the same depths. Many hold fast their integrity, choosing to suffer rather than to sin. This class especially demand help, sympathy, and encouragement.—*The Ministry of Healing,* pp. 189, 190. (1905)

Poor Often Know Not Where to Turn for Relief.— There are multitudes struggling with poverty, compelled to labor hard for small wages, unable to secure the barest necessities of life. Toil and deprivation, with no hope of better things, make their burden heavy. When pain and sickness are added, the burden is almost unbearable. Care-worn and oppressed, they know not where to turn for relief.—*Testimonies for the Church,* vol. 9, p. 90. (1909)

EXPLOITATION OF POOR BY RICH

Rich Become Wealthy by Oppressing Others.—The enemy has succeeded in perverting justice and in filling men's hearts with the desire for selfish gain. "Justice standeth afar off: for truth is fallen in the street, and equity cannot enter" (Isaiah 59:14). In the great cities there are multitudes living in poverty and wretchedness, well nigh destitute of food, shelter, and clothing; while in the same cities are those who have more than heart could wish, who live luxuriously, spending their money on richly furnished houses, on personal adornment, or worse still, upon the gratification of sensual appetites, upon liquor, tobacco, and other things that destroy the powers of the brain, unbalance the mind, and debase the soul. The cries of starving humanity are coming up before God, while by every species of oppression and extortion men are piling up colossal fortunes.—*Testimonies for the Church,* vol. 9, pp. 11, 12. (1909)

God Forbids Enriching Self Through Exploitation of Poor.—God's word sanctions no policy that will enrich one class by the oppression and suffering of another. In all our business transactions it teaches us to put ourselves in the place of those with whom we are dealing, to look not only on our own things, but also on the things of others. He who would take advantage of another's misfortunes in order to benefit himself, or who seeks to profit himself through another's weakness or incompetence, is a transgressor both of the principles and of the precepts of the word of God.—*The Ministry of Healing*, p. 187. (1905)

Sabbatical Year and Jubilee Promoted Social Equality.— The Lord would place a check upon the inordinate love of property and power. Great evils would result from the continued accumulation of wealth by one class, and the poverty and degradation of another. Without some restraint the power of the wealthy would become a monopoly, and the poor, though in every respect fully as worthy in God's sight, would be regarded and treated as inferior to their more prosperous brethren.

The sense of this oppression would arouse the passions of the poorer class. There would be a feeling of despair and desperation which would tend to demoralize society and open the door to crimes of every description. The regulations that God established were designed to promote social equality. The provisions of the sabbatical year and the jubilee would, in a great measure, set right that which during the interval had gone wrong in the social and political economy of the nation.—*Patriarchs and Prophets*, p. 534. (1890)

SOME GIVE HELP

Compassionate Help the Poor.— There are largehearted men and women who are anxiously considering the condition of the poor and what means can be found for their relief. How the unemployed and the homeless can be helped to secure the common blessings of God's providence and to live the life He intended man to live is a question to which many are earnestly endeavoring to find an answer. But there are not many, even among educators and statesmen, who comprehend the causes that underlie the present state of society. Those who hold the reins of government are unable to solve the problem of poverty, pauperism, and increasing crime. They are struggling in vain to place business operations on a more secure basis.—*The Ministry of Healing,* p. 183. (1905)

TRADE UNIONS

Unions Contribute to Increasing Difficulties in Cities.—Through the working of trusts, and the results of labor unions and strikes, the conditions of life in the city are constantly becoming more and more difficult. Serious troubles are before us; and for many families removal from the cities will become a necessity.—*The Ministry of Healing,* p. 364. (1905)

Workers Endangered From Unions.—In all our great cities there will be a binding up in bundles by the confederacies and unions formed. Man will rule other men and demand much of them. The lives of those who refuse to unite with these unions will be in peril. Everything is being prepared for the last great work to be done by the One mighty to save and mighty to destroy.—Manuscript 145, 1902 (*Manuscript Releases,* vol. 3, p. 42).

Union Membership Prevents Keeping the Decalogue.—These unions are one of the signs of the last days. Men are binding up in bundles ready to be burned. They may be church members, but while they belong to these unions, they cannot possibly keep the commandments of God; for to belong to these unions means to disregard the entire Decalogue.—Letter 26, 1903 (*Maranatha,* p. 182).

Among Satan's Final Efforts Is Formation of Unions.—The forming of these unions is one of Satan's last efforts. God calls upon His people to get out of the cities, isolating themselves from the world. The time will come when they will have to do this. God will care for those who love Him and keep His commandments.—Letter 26, 1903 (*Manuscript Releases,* vol. 3, p. 43).

TAINTED BY POPULAR CULTURE

Resources Wasted on Worthless Amusements.—Life in the cities is false and artificial. The intense passion for money getting, the whirl of excitement and pleasure seeking, the thirst for display, the luxury and extravagance, all are forces that, with the great masses of mankind, are turning the mind from life's true purpose. They are opening the door to a thousand evils. Upon the youth they have almost irresistible power.

One of the most subtle and dangerous temptations that assail the children and youth in the cities is the love of pleasure. Holidays are numerous; games and horse racing draw thousands, and the whirl of excitement and pleasure attracts them away from the sober duties of life. Money that should have been saved for better uses is frittered away for amusements.—*The Ministry of Healing,* p. 364. (1905)

Cities Becoming Like Sodom and Gomorrah.—The cities of today are fast becoming like Sodom and Gomorrah. The many holidays encourage idleness. The exciting sports—theatergoing, horse racing, gambling, liquor-drinking, and reveling—stimulate every passion to intense activity. The youth are swept away by the popular current. Those who learn to love amusement for its own sake open the door to a flood of temptations. They give themselves up to social gaiety* and thoughtless mirth, and their intercourse† with pleasure lovers has an intoxicating effect upon the mind. They are led on from one form of dissipation to another, until they lose both the desire and the capacity for a life of usefulness. Their religious aspirations are chilled; their spiritual life is darkened. All the

---

* Nineteenth-century definition: merrymaking, festivity.
† Nineteenth-century definition: communication, interaction.

nobler faculties of the soul, all that link man with the spiritual world, are debased.—*Christ's Object Lessons,* pp. 54, 55. (1900)

Freedom of Individual Action Not Respected.—The very atmosphere of these cities is full of poisonous malaria. The freedom of individual action is not respected; a man's time is not regarded as really his own; he is expected to do as others do. . . .

The devotion to amusements and the observance of so many holidays give a large business to the courts, to officers and judges, and increase the poverty and squalor that need no increasing.—*Special Testimonies on Education,* p. 88. (1897)

Unsupervised Children Form Hurtful Associations.—Parents flock with their families to the cities because they fancy it easier to obtain a livelihood there than in the country. The children, having nothing to do when not in school, obtain a street education. From evil associates they acquire habits of vice and dissipation. The parents see all this; but it will require a sacrifice to correct their error, and they stay where they are until Satan gains full control of their children.—*Testimonies for the Church,* vol. 5, p. 232. (1882)

ENVIRONMENTAL POLLUTION

Pollution Often Imperils Health.—The physical surroundings in the cities are often a peril to health. The constant liability to contact with disease, the prevalence of foul air, impure water, impure food, the crowded, dark, unhealthful dwellings, are some of the many evils to be met. It was not God's purpose that people should be crowded into cities, huddled together in terraces and tenements.—*The Ministry of Healing,* p. 365. (1905)

City Environment Compounds Health Problems for Sick.—The noise and excitement and confusion of the cities, their constrained and artificial life, are most wearisome and exhausting to the sick. The air, laden with smoke and dust, with poisonous gases, and with germs of disease, is a peril to life. The sick, for the most part shut within four walls, come almost to feel as if they were prisoners in their rooms. They look out on houses and pavements and hurrying crowds, with perhaps not even a glimpse of blue sky or sunshine, of grass or flower or tree. Shut up in this way, they brood over their suffering and sorrow, and become a prey to their own sad thoughts.

And for those who are weak in moral power, the cities abound in dangers. In them, patients who have unnatural appetites to overcome are continually exposed to temptation. They need to be placed amid new surroundings where the current of their thoughts will be changed; they need to be placed under influences wholly different from those that have wrecked their lives. Let them for a season be removed from those influences that lead away from God, into a purer atmosphere.—*The Ministry of Healing,* pp. 262, 263. (1905)

CRIME AND CORRUPTION

An "Epidemic of Crime" Exists Everywhere.—We are living in the midst of an "epidemic of crime," at which thoughtful, God-fearing men everywhere stand aghast. The corruption that prevails, it is beyond the power of the human pen to describe. Every day brings fresh revelations of political strife, bribery, and fraud. Every day brings its heart-sickening record of violence and lawlessness, of indifference to human suffering, of brutal, fiendish destruction of human life. Every day testifies to the increase of insanity, murder, and suicide. Who can doubt that satanic agencies are at work among men with increasing activity to distract and corrupt the mind, and defile and destroy the body?

And while the world is filled with these evils, the gospel is too often presented in so indifferent a manner as to make but little impression upon the consciences or the lives of men. Everywhere there are hearts crying out for something which they have not.—*The Ministry of Healing,* pp. 142, 143. (1905)

Cities Worldwide Full of Crime.—The world over, cities are becoming hotbeds of vice. On every hand are the sights and sounds of evil. Everywhere are enticements to sensuality and dissipation. The tide of corruption and crime is continually swelling. Every day brings the record of violence—robberies, murders, suicides, and crimes unnamable.—*The Ministry of Healing,* p. 363. (1905)

Increased Crime Results From Rejection of God.—There is coming rapidly and surely an almost universal guilt upon the inhabitants of the cities, because of the steady increase of determined wickedness. . . .

From age to age Satan has sought to keep men in ignorance of the beneficent designs of Jehovah. He has endeavored to remove from their sight the great things of God's law—the principles of justice, mercy, and love therein set forth. Men boast of the wonderful progress and enlightenment of the age in which we are now living; but God sees the earth filled with iniquity and violence. Men declare that the law of God has been abrogated, that the Bible is not authentic; and as a result, a tide of evil, such as has not been seen since the days of Noah and of apostate Israel, is sweeping over the world. Nobility of soul, gentleness, piety, are bartered away to gratify the lust for forbidden things. The black record of crime committed for the sake of gain is enough to chill the blood and fill the soul with horror.

Our God is a God of mercy. With long-sufferance and tender compassion He deals with the transgressors of His law. And yet, in this our day, when men and women have so many opportunities for becoming familiar with the divine law as revealed in Holy Writ, the great Ruler of the universe cannot behold with any satisfaction the wicked cities, where reign violence and crime. The end of God's forbearance with those who persist in disobedience is approaching rapidly.—*Prophets and Kings,* pp. 275, 276. (1917)

Crime in Cities Continually Increasing.—The youth of our cities breathe in the tainted, polluted atmosphere of crime. The evil influence is then communicated to the country, and the whole community becomes contaminated. The rulers are not men of moral worth, but men who are well supplied with this world's goods, and they have neither the desire nor the inclination to check the growth of this root of bitterness which is increasing year by year, and is fostered and fed by just such publications as are now being sold everywhere, and by such stories and descriptions of criminal practices as are found in the papers of the day.—Manuscript 13, 1895 (*Manuscript Releases,* vol. 10, p. 226).

God Looks With Tenderness Upon Youthful Evildoers.—They see them* enfeebled, dilapidated, without moral force, moral wrecks to communicate their evil practices to others. Parents' hearts are broken. Brothers and sisters and relatives speak of these poor souls as hopeless, but God looks upon them with . . . sorrow and tenderness. He understands all the circumstances which have led them into temptation, which have separated them from God. How can the youth of this generation escape the terrible dishonor of wasting their inheritance given them of God, selling their birthright as did Esau . . . , betraying sacred interests entrusted to them for the blessing of humanity? They indulge in intemperate appetites and through greed to obtain money fall into dishonest practices.

These poor souls need to be brought into connection with high, pure, Bible principles. But first the restoration work must commence in giving them healthful food, and furnishing them facilities for clean bodies and clean clothing, and some sparks of gratitude will begin to flash forth.—Manuscript 14a, 1897.

GOD'S JUDGMENT ON THE CITIES

Lawbreaking Brings God's Judgments.—While at Loma Linda, California, April 16, 1906, there passed before me a most wonderful representation. During a vision of the night, I stood on

---

* [Adults and other youth see youthful evildoers as] "enfeebled, dilapidated, without moral force."

an eminence, from which I could see houses shaken like a reed in the wind. Buildings, great and small, were falling to the ground. Pleasure resorts, theaters, hotels, and the homes of the wealthy were shaken and shattered. Many lives were blotted out of existence, and the air was filled with the shrieks of the injured and the terrified.

The destroying angels of God were at work. One touch, and buildings, so thoroughly constructed that men regarded them as secure against every danger, quickly became heaps of rubbish. There was no assurance of safety in any place. I did not feel in any special peril, but the awfulness of the scenes that passed before me I cannot find words to describe. It seemed that the forbearance of God was exhausted and that the judgment day had come.

The angel that stood at my side then instructed me that but few have any conception of the wickedness existing in our world today, and especially the wickedness in the large cities. He declared that the Lord has appointed a time when He will visit transgressors in wrath for persistent disregard of His law.

Terrible as was the representation that passed before me, that which impressed itself most vividly upon my mind was the instruction given in connection with it. The angel that stood by my side declared that God's supreme rulership and the sacredness of His law must be revealed to those who persistently refused to render obedience to the King of kings. Those who choose to remain disloyal must be visited in mercy with judgments, in order that, if possible, they may be aroused to a realization of the sinfulness of their course.—*Testimonies for the Church,* vol. 9, pp. 92, 93. (1909)

Wickedness Not Restricted to Any Specific City.—Consider the city of San Francisco. What was it that brought the judgments of God upon that city? We read the answer in the revelations that have been made of corruption in those who stood in high office. Corruption and drunkenness and robbery are discovered on every hand. And this condition of wickedness is not in San Francisco alone. We who have the truth understand the meaning of these conditions and events.

We are living in the last evening of this earth's history. Is it not time that every soul place himself in right relation to God to act an individual part for the upbuilding of the kingdom of Christ?—Manuscript 73, 1909 (*Sermons and Talks,* vol. 2, pp. 314, 315).

SENSATIONAL CLAIMS HINDER CITY EVANGELISM

Startling Claims Not to Be Made.—"Not many years ago, a brother laboring in New York City published some very startling notices regarding the destruction of that city. I wrote immediately to the ones in charge of the work there, saying that it was not wise to publish such notices; that thus an excitement might be aroused which would result in a fanatical movement, hurting the cause of God. It is enough to present the truth of the word of God to the people. Startling notices are detrimental to the progress of the work." . . .

"Now comes the word that I have declared that New York is to be swept away by a tidal wave. This I have never said. I have said, as I looked at the great buildings going up there, story after story: 'What terrible scenes will take place when the Lord shall arise to shake terribly the earth! Then the words of Rev. 18:1-3 will be fulfilled.' The whole of the eighteenth chapter of Revelation is a warning of what is coming on the earth. But I have no light in particular in regard to what is coming on New York, only I know that one day the great buildings there will be thrown down by the turning and overturning of God's power. From the light given me, I know that destruction is in the world. One word from the Lord, one touch of His mighty power, and these massive structures will fall. Scenes will take place the fearfulness of which we cannot imagine." . . .

"There are many with whom the Spirit of God is striving. The time of God's destructive judgments is the time of mercy for those who have no opportunity to learn what is truth. Tenderly will the Lord look upon them. His heart of mercy is touched; His hand is still stretched out to save." . . .

"When I was last in New York, I was in the night season called upon to behold buildings rising story after story toward heaven. These buildings were warranted to be fireproof, and they were erected to glorify the owners. Higher and still higher these buildings rose, and in them the most costly material was used. . . .

"As these lofty buildings went up, the owners rejoiced with ambitious pride that they had money to use in glorifying self. . . . Much of the money that they thus invested had been obtained through exaction, through grinding the faces of the poor. In the books of heaven, an account of every business transaction is kept. There every unjust deal, every fraudulent act, is recorded. The time is coming when in their fraud and insolence men will reach a point that the Lord will not permit them to pass, and they will learn that there is a limit to the forbearance of Jehovah.

"The scene that next passed before me was an alarm of fire. Men looked at lofty and supposedly fireproof buildings, and said, 'They are perfectly safe.' But these buildings were consumed as if made of pitch. The fire engines could do nothing to stay the destruction. The firemen were unable to operate the engines.

"I am instructed that when the Lord's time comes, should no change have taken place in the hearts of proud, ambitious human beings, men will find that the hand that has been strong to save will be strong to destroy. No earthly power can stay the hand of God. No material can be used in the erection of buildings that will preserve them from destruction when God's appointed time comes to send retribution on men for their insolence and their disregard of His law."—*Life Sketches of Ellen G. White,* pp. 411-414. (1915; extracts from 1903, 1904, 1906)

Chapter 4

TOTAL INVOLVEMENT NEEDED

BURDEN FOR THE CITIES

Work to Proceed With Great Power.—Our cities are to be worked. To devote our efforts to other worthy enterprises, and leave unworked our cities, in which are large numbers of all nationalities, is not wise. A beginning is now to be made, and means must be raised that the work may go forward. With mighty power the cry is again to be sounded in our large centers of population. . . .

Money is needed for the prosecution of the work in New York, Boston, Portland [Maine], Philadelphia, Buffalo, Chicago, St. Louis, New Orleans, and many other cities. In some of these places the people were mightily stirred by the message given in 1842 to 1844, but of late years little has been done compared to the great work that ought to be in progress. And it seems difficult to make our people feel a special burden for the work in the large cities.—Manuscript 13, 1910 (*A Call to the Watchmen* [Pamphlet 020], p. 4; portions in *Evangelism*, p. 34).

Worldwide Warning to Be Given.—Night after night I am unable to sleep, because of this burden resting upon me in behalf of the unwarned cities. Night after night I am praying and trying to devise methods by which we can enter these cities and give the warning message. Why, there is a world to be warned and saved, and we are to go East and West and North and South, and work intelligently for the people all about us. As we undertake this work, we shall see the salvation of God. Encouragement will come.—Manuscript 53, 1909 (*Evangelism*, p. 62).

Local Work Not to Be Neglected.—Let not the fields lying in the shadow of our doors, such as the great cities in our land, be lightly passed over and neglected. . . . The work in the home field is a *vital problem* just now. The present time is the most favorable opportunity that we shall have to work these fields. In a little while the situation will be much more difficult.—*Testimonies for the Church,* vol. 8, pp. 31, 32. (1904)

Work to Continue Until Close of Probation.—How can we find language to express our deep interest, to describe our desire that every soul should awake and go to work in the Master's vineyard? Christ says, "Occupy till I come." It may be but a few years until our life's history shall close, but we must occupy till then. The fiat will go forth, "He that is unjust, let him be unjust still: and he which is filthy, let him be filthy still: and he that is righteous, let him be righteous still: and he that is holy, let him be holy still," and then there will be no more occasion to labor for souls. Every case will be decided.—*Review and Herald,* April 21, 1896.

TAKE ADVANTAGE OF OPPORTUNITIES

Seize Every Available Opportunity to Work.—God requires that we shall give the message of present truth to every city, and not keep the work bound up in a few places. Wherever an opening for the truth can be found, there let men be stationed who are capable of presenting its teachings with a power and conviction that will reach hearts. . . .

Let none set up as the Lord's way the way of human devisings.

The words were spoken to me with impelling power: Wake up the watchmen to carry the word of warning to every city in America. . . .

Do not hover over the churches to repeat over and over again the same truths to the people, while the cities are left in ignorance and sin, unwarned and unlabored for. Soon the way will be hedged up and these cities will be closed to the gospel message. Wake up the church members, that they may unite in doing a definite and self-denying work.—Manuscript 61, 1909 (*Manuscript Releases,* vol. 10, pp. 215, 216).

Enter When Doors Open.—God asks, Why are not memorials for Me established in the cities? What answer can we return? The neglected work in our cities testifies to the lack of Christlike energy among believers. Let all awake to the need of establishing Christian missions in the cities. Let God's workers enter the doors that He has opened for them. Believers need to arouse and do much more than they are now doing in lines of Christian effort.—*Review and Herald,* February 4, 1904.

Expansion Opportunities Missed.—If during the last twenty years there had been in our large cities aggressive, enthusiastic efforts to proclaim the message of truth, it would have been accepted by thousands who would not only be rejoicing in it, but laboring to impart it to others. . . .

In centers such as Washington* and Mountain View† and Nashville,‡ there should not be an effort to add new responsibilities and gather together more families of believers, but rather our brethren in these places should study how they can move out and establish centers of influence in places where is need of work being done.—Letter 41, 1911.

BEWARE: DOORS ALSO OPEN TO OPPONENTS

Doors Open Both to Mission Work and to Opposers of Truth.—Aggressive warfare must be entered upon with a devoted,

---

* Washington, D.C., location of the General Conference from 1904 to 1989, and the Review and Herald Publishing Association from 1906 to 1982.

† Mountain View, California, location of the Pacific Press Publishing Association from 1904 to 1984.

‡ Nashville, Tennessee, location of the Southern Publishing Association from 1901 to 1980.

self-sacrificing spirit that many know nothing about. As opportunities offer, as doors open, and the word of life is brought to the people, opposition to the truth will start into operation. The door that is open to the missionary will also be open to the opposer of truth. But if the truth is presented as it is in Jesus, the hearers are responsible for its rejection.—*Review and Herald,* July 2, 1895.

INVOLVE MEMBERS IN COMMUNITY MINISTRY

All Called to Awaken to Needs of the Cities.—As they see the unworked cities, our brethren realize the greatness of the work to be done. Many who in the past ought to have been wide awake, giving heed to the messages sent, have been asleep. Our people are now to awake. If all will do their duty, we shall see the work of the Lord carried forward in earnest. May God help us is my prayer.—Letter 102, 1910.

One Hundred Workers Needed Where Now There Is One.—The cities are teeming with iniquity, and Satan suggests that it is impossible to do any good within their borders; and so they are sadly neglected. But there are lost pearls there, whose value you cannot realize until you earnestly seek to find them. There might be one hundred workers where there is but one, who might be seeking diligently, prayerfully, and with intense interest, to find the pearls that are buried in the rubbish of these cities.—*Review and Herald,* April 21, 1896.

MINISTERS CALLED TO CITY EVANGELISM

Ministers to Work Large Cities.—I am instructed to point our ministers to the unworked cities and to urge them by every possible means to open the way for the presentation of the truth. In some of the cities where the message of the second coming of the Lord was first given, we are compelled to take up the work as if it were a new field. How much longer will these barren fields, these unworked cities, be passed by? Without delay the sowing of the seed should begin in many, many places.—*Testimonies for the Church*, vol. 9, p. 123. (1909)

STUDENTS TO PARTICIPATE

Students to Engage in Various Forms of Evangelism.—Through the first disciples a divine gift was proffered to Israel; the faithful evangelist today will do a similar work in every city where our missionaries enter. It is a work which to some extent we have tried to do in connection with some of our sanitariums, but a much wider experience in these lines is to be gained.

Cannot our conference presidents open the way for the students in our schools to engage in this line of labor? Again and again it has been presented to me that "there should be companies organized and educated most thoroughly to work as nurses, as evangelists, as ministers, as canvassers, as gospel students, to perfect a character after the divine similitude."—*Testimonies and Experiences Connected With the Loma Linda Sanitarium and College of Medical Evangelists* (Pamphlet 095), p. 15 (*Counsels on Health*, pp. 541, 542). (1906)

CHURCH LEADERS TO BE INVOLVED

Church Leaders to Assist.—To my brethren in positions of responsibility I would say, the needs of the large cities have been kept before you. You have had message after message concerning your duty. And now what will you do that the charge of the Lord may be obeyed?—Manuscript 13, 1910.

Lateness of Time Requires Prayerful Action Now.—If our leaders realized the time of night, they could not leave our cities unwarned and be willing to do so little to change the present condition of things in the world. God requires that every soul who believes in Christ shall go forth and bear much fruit. . . .

Let there be less sermonizing and more humbling of the soul in prayer for the divine presence among us. Our meetings should be seasons of humble seeking after God. Oh, that we might sense our need of Christ and by living faith claim the promise of His presence!—Letter 172, 1908 (*Spalding and Magan Collection,* p. 436).

Church Leaders Who Neglect the Cities Held Accountable by God.—I am instructed to say to those who have long stood at the head of the work, and who for years have allowed many of our large cities to remain unworked: The Lord will call to account those who have worked out their own plans to do a large work in a few places while they have left undone the work that should have been done in giving the last warning message to the many large cities of our land. There has been with some a spirit of forbidding, a desire to hold back from the work brethren who desired to have a part in it. Some in the blindness of their hearts have been hindering the work, and this has brought unbelief into many hearts. I am now counseled in regard to the need of employing all our energies and all our means for the advancement of the work. We need to use our influence in encouraging others to labor. Let the spirit of sanctified activity be encouraged rather than the spirit that would seek to hinder and forbid, and there will be seen advancement where in the past there has been failure to follow the will of the Lord.— Manuscript 61, 1909 (*Manuscript Releases,* vol. 10, p. 219).

General Conference Leaders Called to Do City Evangelism.—I have seen that Satan would have been greatly pleased to see Elders [W. W.] Prescott and [A. G.] Daniells undertake the work of a general overhauling of our books that have done a good work in the field for years. But neither of you is called of God to that work. If you were to enter upon such a work, much time would be employed that should be given to the proclamation of the last warning message to an impenitent world.

The Lord would have been pleased had you and Elder Prescott and your associates taken upon yourselves soon after the last General Conference the burden of giving to the inhabitants of the great cities the last warning message. This is a work that He has been calling us to do these many years.—Letter 70, 1910 (*Manuscript Releases,* vol. 10, pp. 364, 365).

A General Conference President Called to Do City Evangelism.

—The Lord Jesus says to the president of the General Conference [A. G. Daniells], "My grace is sufficient for thee: for My strength is made perfect in weakness." Warn the cities. Time is precious. Repent, and be converted. Repent, and redeem the time. Let everything be done that can be done to atone for your past neglect. . . .

Elder Daniells, let your heart and mind be wholly consecrated to do the will of God, and labor for a similar work to take place in your family. Take up the long-neglected work in the cities. Plead with God most earnestly to set your mind to running in right channels. The Lord has not laid upon you nor upon anyone else in Washington the work that some have fancied ought to be done.— Letter 70, 1910.

A *Review and Herald* Editor Called to Do City Evangelism.

—During this [1909 General] Conference I had a message for Brother [W. W.] Prescott. He is a minister. He should not remain here in Washington to do a work that another man can do. He can stand before the people and give the reasons of our faith in an acceptable way. I know this because I have been associated with him in labor. He has a precious gift, and here he is employed in work that other men can do, while there is a dearth of laborers who can warn these large cities. His gift is not to be used longer as it is now, for if he continues to labor here, his health and strength will be used up. But if he will go out into the public ministry, strength will come to him.—Manuscript 53, 1909 (*Manuscript Releases,* vol. 10, pp. 360, 361).

MISSION OFFERINGS
NOT A SUBSTITUTE FOR SERVICE

Obligation to Cities Not Met by Giving Mission Offerings.—Unless more is done than has been done for the cities of America, ministers and people will have a heavy account to settle with the One who has appointed to every man his work. . . .

May God forgive our terrible neglect in not doing the work that as yet we have scarcely touched with the tips of our fingers. . . .

After you have given something for foreign fields, do not think your duty done.—*Testimonies for the Church,* vol. 8, pp. 35, 36. (1904)

Chapter 5

A STRATEGY
FOR REACHING THE CITIES

GOD DESIRES SPECIFIC
WORK BE DONE IN CITIES

Great Work Needs to Be Done in Cities.—Again and again I am instructed to present to our churches the work that should be done in our large cities. There is a great work to be done, not only where we have churches already established, but also in places where the truth has never been fully presented. Right in our midst there are heathen as verily as in far-off lands.—Manuscript 7, 1908 (*Evangelism*, p. 32).

Do Not Wait for Something Large to Happen Before Starting.—Why should we delay to begin work in our cities? We are not to wait for some wonderful thing to be done, or some costly apparatus to be provided, in order that a great display may be made. What is the chaff to the wheat? If we walk and work humbly before God, He will prepare the way before us. He will honor those who honor Him. And we feel sure that the workmen at Takoma Park* are seeking to honor Him.

Why delay the endeavor to make the world better? However humble our sphere, however lowly our work, if we walk in harmony with our Saviour, He will reveal Himself through us, and our influence will draw souls to Him. He will honor the meek and lowly

---

* Takoma Park, a suburb of Washington, D.C., location of the General Conference, 1904 to 1989; location of the Review and Herald Publishing Association, 1906 to 1982.

ones, who earnestly seek to do service for Him in the daily life. Into all that we do, whether we work in the shop, on the farm, or in the office, let us bring the endeavor to save souls.—Letter 335, 1904.

Special Talent Exists to Accomplish Work.—Mission work should be done in all our large cities. There is special talent among us for this line of labor, and this talent should be educated and trained.

The ministers who hover over the churches are accomplishing little good for church members unless they encourage and teach the people to do practical missionary work. Every minister should now feel that there is a greater work for him to do than to repeat again and again the same sermons to the people. . . .

I have been instructed to refer our people to the fifty-eighth chapter of Isaiah. Read this chapter carefully, and understand the kind of ministry that will bring life into the churches. The work of the gospel is to be carried by means of our liberality as well as by our labors. When you meet suffering souls who need help, give it to them. When you find those who are hungry, feed them. In doing this you will be working in lines of Christ's ministry. . . .

It is not the duty of conference officers to lay restraining hands on the work being done in our cities. By the strange forbiddings that have been exercised in some places, Satan has been seeking to hedge up the way of the truth. The people need no encouragement to inactivity.—Manuscript 7, 1908.

Best Workers to Be Chosen.—We must labor now for the extension of the truth, and as a result many souls will come to a knowledge of the truth in our hitherto unworked cities. The very choicest instrumentalities the church contains should be selected and sent forth, and sustained in extending missionary efforts.—*Atlantic Union Gleaner,* January 8, 1902.

Workers Needed Who Can Reach People's Hearts.—We must plan to place in these great cities capable men who can present the third angel's message in a manner so forceful that it will strike home to the heart. Men who can do this, we cannot afford to gather into one place, to do a work that others might do.—*Review and Herald,* November 25, 1909.

CONFUSION REGARDING HOW TO WORK THE CITIES

Satan Attempts to Confuse Our Plans.—As we begin active work for the multitudes in the cities, the enemy will work mightily to bring in confusion, hoping thus to break up the working forces. Some who are not thoroughly converted are in constant danger of mistaking the suggestions of the enemy as the leadings of the Spirit of God. As the Lord has given us light, let us walk in the light.—Manuscript 13, 1910 (*Evangelism,* p. 100).

Excuses for Not Doing City Evangelism Demonstrate Lack of Vision.—I dreamed that several of our brethren were in counsel considering plans of labor for this season. They thought it best not to enter the large cities, but to begin work in small places, remote from the cities; here they would meet less opposition from the clergy and would avoid great expense. They reasoned that our ministers, being few in number, could not be spared to instruct and care for those who might accept the truth in the cities, and who, because of the greater opposition they would there meet, would need more help than would the churches in small country places. Thus the fruit of giving a course of lectures in the city would, in a great measure, be lost. Again, it was urged that, because of our limited means, and because of the many changes from moving that might be expected from a church in a large city, it would be difficult to build up a church that would be a strength to the cause. My husband was urging the brethren to make broader plans without delay and put forth, in our large cities, extended and thorough effort that would better correspond to the character of our message. One worker related incidents of his experience in the cities, showing that the work was nearly a failure, but he testified to better success in the small places.

One of dignity and authority—One who is present in all our council meetings—was listening with deepest interest to every word. He spoke with deliberation and perfect assurance. "The whole world," He said, "is God's great vineyard. The cities and villages constitute a part of that vineyard. These must be worked." ...

The Messenger turned to one present and said: "Your ideas of the work for this time are altogether too limited. Your light must not be confined to a small compass, put under a bushel, or under a bed; it must be placed on a candlestick, that it may give light to all that are in God's house—the world. You must take broader views of the work than you have taken."—*Testimonies for the Church*, vol. 7, pp. 34-36 (similar to Manuscript 1, 1874).

CHRIST'S METHOD FOR REACHING THE CITIES

Mingle With People, Meet Their Needs, Then Invite Them to Follow.—When Christ sent out the twelve disciples on their first missionary tour, He bade them, "As ye go, preach, saying, The kingdom of heaven is at hand. Heal the sick, cleanse the lepers, raise the dead, cast out devils: freely ye have received, freely give" (Matthew 10:7, 8).

To the Seventy sent forth later He said: "Into whatsoever city ye enter, ... heal the sick that are therein, and say unto them, The kingdom of God is come nigh unto you" (Luke 10:8, 9). ...

After Christ's ascension the same work was continued. The scenes of His own ministry were repeated. ...

Luke, the writer of the Gospel that bears his name, was a medical missionary. In the Scriptures he is called "the beloved physician" (Colossians 4:14). The apostle Paul heard of his skill as a physician, and sought him out as one to whom the Lord had entrusted a special work. He secured his cooperation, and for some time Luke accompanied him in his travels from place to place. ... Thus the way was opened for the gospel message. Luke's success as a physician gained for him many opportunities for preaching Christ among the heathen. It is the divine plan that we shall work as the disciples worked. Physical healing is bound up with the gospel commission. In the work of the gospel, teaching and healing are never to be separated. . . .

The giving of the gospel to the world is the work that God has committed to those who bear His name. For earth's sin and misery the gospel is the only antidote. To make known to all mankind the message of the grace of God is the first work of those who know its healing power. . . .

What is the condition in the world today? Is not faith in the Bible as effectually destroyed by the higher criticism and speculation? . . .

A great work of reform is demanded, and it is only through the grace of Christ that the work of restoration, physical, mental, and spiritual, can be accomplished.

Christ's method alone will give true success in reaching the people. The Saviour mingled with men as one who desired their good. He showed His sympathy for them, ministered to their needs, and won their confidence. Then He bade them, "Follow Me."

There is need of coming close to the people by personal effort. If less time were given to sermonizing, and more time were spent in personal ministry, greater results would be seen. The poor are to be relieved, the sick cared for, the sorrowing and the bereaved comforted, the ignorant instructed, the inexperienced counseled. We are to weep with those that weep, and rejoice with those that rejoice. Accompanied by the power of persuasion, the power of prayer, the power of the love of God, this work will not, cannot, be without fruit.—*The Ministry of Healing,* pp. 139-144. (1905)

Christ Came to Meet the Needs of Humanity.—God sent His Son into the world that He might learn by actual experience the needs of humanity. Through humanity combined with divinity

He must reach man and enable him to lay hold upon the divine nature.—Manuscript 73, 1909 (*Sermons and Talks,* vol. 2, p. 318).

ACTIONS OF CITY WORKERS IMPORTANT

Character of Work to Match Truths We Teach.—The work should be symmetrical, and a living witness for the truth. God would have us cherish a noble ambition. He desires that the character of our work shall be in harmony with the great truths we are agitating to awaken the world from its deathlike slumber.—Letter 4, 1899.

Teach by Example.—We must live the truth, and teach it by our lives as well as by our words. There are thousands within our reach to whom we can teach the truth, and it does not require the investment of large means to reach our neighboring towns and cities. We do not need to go to a people of a strange town, but to English-speaking people, and yet year after year has passed by, appeal after appeal has been sent out, and yet men, women, and means have done little to advance the work. Are we the light of the world?—Manuscript 60, 1894.

AVOID CONTENTIOUS ACTIONS

Avoid Needlessly Building Walls of Separation.—The Lord does not move upon His workers to make them take a course which will bring on the time of trouble before the time. Let them not build up a wall of separation between themselves and the world, by advancing their own ideas and notions. There is now altogether too much of this throughout our borders.—*Special Testimonies to Ministers and Workers,* Series A, No. 3, pp. 33, 34 (*Testimonies to Ministers and Gospel Workers,* p. 202). (1895)

STRATEGIC PLANNING

City Dwellers Will Not Come to Us.—Can we expect the

inhabitants of the cities to come to us and say: "If you will come to us and preach, we will help you to do thus and so"? What do they know of our message? Let us do our part in warning these people who are ready to perish unwarned and unsaved. The Lord desires us to let our light so shine before men that His Holy Spirit can communicate the truth to the honest in heart who are seeking after Him.—*Testimonies for the Church,* vol. 9, p. 100. (1909)

Study Outreach Possibilities.—The words were spoken to me: "Tell My people that time is short. Every effort is now to be made to exalt the truth. In the cities, large and small, the message is to be proclaimed. The third angel's message is to be united with the second angel's message, and is to be proclaimed with great power in our large cities. Thus will be given with a loud voice the message that is to prepare a people for the coming of the King."

The situation in all the large cities must be studied, that the truth may be given to all the people. In these large cities the Lord has many honest souls who are becoming confused by the strange developments in the religious world.—Letter 88, 1910 (*Manuscript Releases,* vol. 5, p. 128).

Needs of Neglected Areas to Be Studied.—There is another line of work to be carried forward, the work in the large cities. There should be companies of earnest laborers working in the cities. Men should study what needs to be done in the places that have been neglected. The Lord has been calling our attention to the neglected multitudes in the large cities, yet little regard has been given to the matter.—*Review and Herald,* November 11, 1909 (*Fundamentals of Christian Education,* p. 537).

Careful Planning by Several Helps Prevent Mistakes.— Capable men are needed who will carefully count the cost and use sound judgment in their calculations. The lack of experienced men has been a great disadvantage. . . . The work should not be managed by one man's mind or by one man's ideas. . . .

It would be a mistake to build or purchase large buildings in the cities. . . . Those who seem to see such great advantages in so doing are without understanding.

There is a great work to be done in sounding the gospel message for this time in these large cities, but the fitting up of large buildings for some apparently wonderful work has been a mistake.—Manuscript 30, 1903 (*Sermons and Talks,* vol. 2, p. 226).

Poor Planning Results in Unnecessary Expenditures.— I have been much pained because means have been invested in putting up additional school buildings at Battle Creek, when this was uncalled for. The college was large enough to accommodate the students that could be managed successfully in the school. The fact of the matter was that those in charge were not able to manage the students that were already in attendance as they should be managed, and the money invested in putting up new buildings was greatly needed in planting the standard of truth in cities in America, and in opening new fields to the living minister.—Letter 43, 1895 (*Manuscript Releases,* vol. 17, p. 308).

LOCAL LEADERSHIP NEEDED

Decisions Regarding Local Work Best Made Locally.— I am often greatly distressed when I see our leading men taking extreme positions, and burdening themselves over matters that should not be taken up or worried over, but left in the hands of God for Him to adjust. We are yet in the world, and God keeps for us a place in connection with the world, and works by His own right hand to prepare the way before us, in order that His work may progress along its various lines. . . .

Let the Lord work with the men who are on the ground, and let those who are not on the ground walk humbly with God, lest they get out of their place, and lose their bearings. The Lord has not placed the burden of criticizing the work upon those who have taken this burden, and He does not give them the sanction of His

Holy Spirit. Many move according to their own human judgment, and zealously seek to adjust things that God has not placed in their hands. Just as long as we are in the world, we shall have to do a special work for the world; the message of warning is to go to all countries, tongues, and peoples.—*Special Testimonies to Ministers and Workers,* Series A, No. 3, pp. 32, 33 (*Testimonies to Ministers and Gospel Workers,* pp. 201, 202). (1895)

FUNDING CITY EVANGELISM

Money and Talents Both Needed in God's Work.—Those who are truly converted are called to do a work which requires money and consecration. The obligations which bind us to place our names on the church roll hold us responsible to work to the utmost of our ability for God. He calls for undivided service, for the entire devotion of heart, soul, mind, and strength. Christ has brought us into church capacity, that He may engage and engross all our capabilities in devoted service for the salvation of others. Anything short of this is opposition to the work. . . .

The Lord designs that the means entrusted to us shall be used in building up His kingdom. His goods are committed to His stewards, that they may be carefully traded upon, and bring back a revenue to Him in the saving of souls unto eternal life. . . .

God works with every true believer, and the light and blessing received is given out again in the work which the believer does. As he thus gives of that which he has received, his capacity for receiving is increased. As he imparts of the heavenly gifts, he makes room for fresh currents of grace and truth to flow into the soul from the living fountain. Greater light, increased knowledge and blessing, are his. In this work, which devolves upon every church member, is the life and growth of the church.

He whose life consists in ever receiving and never giving soon loses the blessing. If truth does not flow forth from him to others, he loses his capacity to receive.—Manuscript 139, 1898 (*This Day With God,* p. 303).

Needed Finances Will Come.—As we do this work, we shall find that means will flow into our treasuries, and we shall have means with which to carry on a still broader and more far-reaching work. Shall we not advance in faith, just as if we had thousands of dollars? We do not have half faith enough. Let us act our part in warning these cities.—Manuscript 53, 1909 (*Evangelism,* p. 62).

Members With Financial Resources to Support Outreach Efforts.—The Lord calls upon those who are in positions of trust, those to whom He has entrusted His precious gifts, to use their talents of intellect and means in His service. Our workers should present before these men a plain statement of our plan of labor, telling them what we need in order to help the poor and needy and to establish this work on a firm basis. Some of these will be impressed by the Holy Spirit to invest the Lord's means in a way that will advance His cause. They will fulfill His purpose by helping to create centers of influence in the large cities. Interested workers will be led to offer themselves for various lines of missionary effort.—*Testimonies for the Church,* vol. 7, p. 112. (1902)

Wealthy Converts Will Help Fund City Evangelism.—Souls who have wealth will be brought into the truth and will give of their means to advance the work of God. I have been instructed that there is much means in the cities that are unworked. God has interested people there. Go to them; teach them as Christ taught; give them the truth. They will accept it. And as surely as honest souls will be converted, their means will be consecrated to the Lord's service, and we shall see an increase of resources.—*Testimonies for the Church,* vol. 9, p. 100. (1909)

FUNDS FOR CHURCH PLANTING
TO BE BUDGETED

Conferences to Reserve Funds for Use in New Fields.—As we consider the work that must be done in Washington [D.C.]

City, and the varied lines of work that should be taken up in the Southern field and in the cities of our land, it is becoming more and more manifest that it is unwise to allow our conferences to be [so] stripped of means that they cannot assist in establishing memorials in fields where God has instructed us to do a special work.—Letter 190, 1903 (*Spalding and Magan Collection,* p. 316).

Financial Priority Given to Opening New Fields.—God requires that every available dollar shall be given to the work of opening new fields for the entrance of the gospel message and in lessening the mountains of difficulty that seek to close up our missionary work. For Christ's sake, I ask you to carry out God's purposes for the opening of missions in every city, in every place.—Manuscript 61, 1909 (*Manuscript Releases,* vol. 10, pp. 216, 217).

Allocate More Funds to New Fields.—Carry the message into new cities. If necessary, we must expend less means in the few places where the message has been quite fully preached, that we may go out into other places where the warning has not been given, and where men and women are ignorant of the great crisis that is about to come to all who live upon the earth. We have the word of truth—the commandments of God and the faith of Jesus—to give to the people of this generation.—Manuscript 61, 1909 (*Manuscript Releases,* vol. 10, p. 216).

Balanced Funding Needed Between Current and New Work.—The Lord sees the work that must be done in His vineyard. He sees the places in which there should be memorials for Him, in order that the truth may be represented. He sees the fields that are unworked and destitute of facilities. He requires from all who serve Him equity and just judgment. A large amount of means should not be absorbed in one place. Every building erected is to be erected with reference to the other places that will need similar buildings. . . .

God calls upon those who act a part in His service not to block the way of advance by selfishly using in one place or in one line of work all the means they can secure. In all parts of the world there is a work to be done that ought to have been done long ago. God forbid that you should make appeals to the people for means to complete . . . [more buildings for a certain institution], when you already have many buildings in your possession, and when you have thousands of dollars in sight. Bring your building to your means. Give other parts of God's vineyard a chance to have facilities. Let plants be made in other cities.—*Special Testimonies,* Series B, No. 6, p. 40. (1908)

Dividing Staff Weakens Work in Both Places.—In the night season I was in a council meeting where Brother Smith Sharp was speaking of dividing the working force at Nashville [Tennessee] and taking part of it to Chattanooga [Tennessee]. Several other matters were introduced. Then the Counsellor* who never makes a mistake spoke words which changed the whole atmosphere of the meeting. He laid down principles which showed that the working forces were not to be divided. That which is needed to make one center should not be used to make two centers. Put all the force into one center, and unite to make that center a success. Nashville is to be made a center, and from it light will radiate to the regions beyond. Should the suggestions urged by Brother Smith Sharp be followed, two sets of buildings would have to be put up, when there is scarcely financial strength to make one place a success. To try to separate the work and establish it in two places would weaken the force of both. Make the work in one place as complete a whole as possible.—Letter 79, 1901.

Use of Funds to Be Guided by Equity, Justice, and Judgment.—Unduly to invest means and exalt this work in one part of the field when there is city work to be done in many places is not the right thing. It is selfishness and covetousness. The Lord especially condemns such a manifestation, for by it His sacred work is misrep-

---

* See Isaiah 9:6.

resented before the world. He would have His work controlled and guided by equity, justice, and judgment. He does not call for the erection of immense institutions. One corner of the vineyard is not the whole world. In many places throughout the world memorials for God are to be established to represent His truth. And such a reasonable course is to be pursued that we shall stand in our large cities in so sensible an attitude that those not of our faith will give us help with their means. Every dollar that we have belongs to God. "The silver is mine, and the gold is mine, saith the Lord of hosts" (Haggai 2:8).

Yet some do not recognize His ownership. Though the work in the part of the field where they are laboring already possesses an abundance of facilities, they continue to draw from the Lord's treasury. They do not think of the needy portions of the field, which require such facilities as they already have, and must be helped. Would they work as zealously to provide for some other place the facilities they think are required in their field? All must consider there are cities that have never had the message.—Manuscript 53, 1903 (*Manuscript Releases,* vol. 13, pp. 406, 407).

Jealousy Over Funds Prevents Work From Progressing.— For years the work in the cities has been presented before me, and has been urged upon our people. Instruction has been given to open new fields. There has sometimes been a jealous fear lest someone who wished to enter new fields should receive means from the people that they supposed was wanted for another work. Some in responsible positions have felt that nothing should be done without their personal knowledge and approval. Therefore efficient workers have been sometimes delayed and hindered, and the carriage wheels of progress in entering new fields have been made to move heavily.—Manuscript 21, 1910 (*Medical Ministry,* p. 302).

FINANCIAL DETAILS NOT THE FOCUS OF PASTORS

Ministers Not to Be Burdened With Financial Details of City Work.—I do not know when our ministers will learn to let business and financial matters alone. Over and over again I have been shown that this is not the work of the ministry. They are not to be heavily burdened with the details of city work. They are to be in readiness to go to places where an interest has been awakened in the message, and especially to attend our camp meetings. They are not to hover over cities at the time when these meetings are in progress.—Manuscript 104, 1902 (*Manuscript Releases,* vol. 17, p. 52).

Chapter 6

NURTURING
AND TRAINING WORKERS

Church Spirituality and Growth Proportionate to Missionary Zeal of Members.—The piety and advanced spiritual knowledge and growth of a church is proportionate to the zeal, piety, and missionary intelligence that has been brought into it, and carried out of it to be a blessing to the very ones who need our assistance the most. Again I urge you to consider Isaiah 58, which opens a wide and extensive vineyard to be worked upon the lines which the Lord has pointed out. When this is done there will be an increase of moral sources, and the church will no more remain almost stationary.— Manuscript 14a, 1897 (*The Seventh-day Adventist Bible Commentary*, Ellen G. White Comments, vol. 4, p. 1148).

Spiritual Growth Results From Active Service.—Every church member should be engaged in some line of service for the Master. Some cannot do so much as others, but everyone should do his utmost to roll back the tide of disease and distress that is sweeping over our world. . . .

Nothing will so arouse a self-sacrificing zeal and broaden and strengthen the character as to engage in work for others. Many professed Christians, in seeking church relationship, think only of themselves. They wish to enjoy church fellowship and pastoral care. They become members of large and prosperous churches, and are content to do little for others. In this way they are robbing themselves of the most precious blessings. . . .

Trees that are crowded closely together do not grow healthfully and sturdily. The gardener transplants them that they may have room to develop. A similar work would benefit many of the members of large churches. They need to be placed where their energies will be called forth in active Christian effort. They are losing their spiritual life, becoming dwarfed and inefficient, for want of self-sacrificing labor for others. Transplanted to some missionary field, they would grow strong and vigorous.

But none need wait until called to some distant field before beginning to help others. Doors of service are open everywhere. All around us are those who need our help. The widow, the orphan, the sick and the dying, the heartsick, the discouraged, the ignorant, and the outcast are on every hand.—*The Ministry of Healing,* pp. 149-152. (1905)

CHRIST, THE PERFECT PATTERN

Christ's Character, Not Just Preaching, Needed.—I attended the morning ministers' meeting.* The blessing of the Lord came upon me, and I spoke in the demonstration of the Spirit of God and with power. There are those who are working out a great circle. The Lord has given Christ to the world for ministry. Merely to preach the Word is not ministry. The Lord desires His ministering servants to occupy a place worthy of the highest consideration. In the mind of God, the ministry of men and women existed before the world was created. He determined that His ministers should have a perfect exemplification of Himself and His purposes. No human career could do this work; for God gave Christ in humanity to work out His ideal of what humanity may become through entire obedience to His will and way. God's character was revealed in the life of His Son. Christ not only held a theory of genuine ministry, but in His humanity He wrought out an illustration of the ministry that God approves. Perfection has marked out every feature of true ministry. Christ, the Son of the living God, did not live unto Himself, but unto God.—Manuscript 23, 1891 (*Manuscript Releases,* vol. 18, p. 380).

---

* Sunday, March 15, 1891, in Battle Creek, Michigan.

Christ Abased Himself to Raise Sinners to Nobler Life.—When we view the generosity of Christ to the poor and suffering, His patience with the rude and ignorant, His self-denial and sacrifice, we are lost in admiration and reverence. What a gift has God lavished upon man, alienated from Him by sin and disobedience! Well may the heart break and the tears flow in contemplation of such inexpressible love! Christ abased Himself to humanity that He might reach man sunken into the depths of woe and degradation, and lift him into a nobler life.—*The Spirit of Prophecy,* vol. 2, p. 286. (1877)

TRAITS FOR EFFECTIVE WITNESSING

Demonstration of Genuine Christianity.—The world needs evidences of sincere Christianity. The poison of sin is at work at the heart of society. Cities and towns are steeped in sin and moral corruption. The world is full of sickness, suffering, and iniquity. Nigh and afar off are souls in poverty and distress, weighed down with a sense of guilt and perishing for want of a saving influence. The gospel of truth is kept ever before them, yet they perish because the example of those who should be a savor of life to them is a savor of death. Their souls drink in bitterness because the springs are poisoned, when they should be like a well of water springing up unto everlasting life.

Salt must be mingled with the substance to which it is added; it must penetrate, infuse it, that it may be preserved. So it is through personal contact and association that men are reached by the saving power of the gospel. They are not saved as masses, but as individuals. Personal influence is a power. It is to work with the influence of Christ, to lift where Christ lifts, to impart correct principles, and to stay the progress of the world's corruption. It is to diffuse that grace which Christ alone can impart. It is to uplift, to sweeten the lives and characters of others by the power of a pure example united with earnest faith and love.—*Prophets and Kings,* p. 232. (1917)

All Selfishness to Be Eradicated.—If Seventh-day Advent

ists will now arouse and do the work assigned them, the truth will be presented to our neglected cities in clear, distinct lines and in the power of the Spirit. When wholehearted work is done, the efficacy of the grace of Christ will be seen. The watchmen on the walls of Zion are to be wide awake, and they are to arouse others. God's people are to be so earnest and faithful in their work for Him that all selfishness will be separated from their lives. His workers will then see eye to eye, and . . . the power of which was seen in the life of Christ, will be revealed. Confidence will be restored, and there will be unity in the churches throughout our ranks.—*Testimonies for the Church,* vol. 9, pp. 32, 33. (1909)

Ministers to Befriend the Poor.—Every gospel minister should be a friend to the poor, the afflicted, and the oppressed among God's believing people. Christ was always the poor man's friend, and the interests of the poor need to be sacredly guarded. There has too often been a wonderful dearth of Christ's compassion and loving interest in the poor and afflicted. Love, sacred, refined love, is to be exercised in behalf of the poor and unfortunate.—Letter 168, 1909 (*Medical Ministry,* p. 310).

EDUCATED WORKERS
ESSENTIAL FOR CITY WORK

Cultivated Intellects, Not Novices, Needed.—Cultivated intellects are now needed in every part of the work of God; for novices cannot do the work acceptably in unfolding the hidden treasure to enrich souls. God has devised that schools shall be an instrumentality for developing workers for Jesus Christ of whom He will not be ashamed, and this object must ever be kept in view. The height man may reach by proper culture has not hitherto been realized. We have among us more than an average of men of ability. If their capabilities were brought into use, we should have twenty ministers where we now have one. Physicians, too, would be educated to battle with disease.—*Special Testimonies to Ministers and*

Workers, Series A, No. 3, p. 22 (*Testimonies to Ministers and Gospel Workers,* p. 195). (1895)

Thoughtful, Prayerful Study of Human Nature Needed.—It requires a knowledge of human nature, close study, careful thought, and earnest prayer, to know how to approach men and women on the great subjects that concern their eternal welfare.—*Gospel Workers,* p. 92. (1915)

Understanding of Humanity Needed.—He who seeks to transform humanity must himself understand humanity. Only through sympathy, faith, and love can men be reached and uplifted.—*Education,* p. 78. (1903)

Mental Culture Needed.—Mental culture is what we as a people need, and what we must have in order to meet the demands of the time.—*Testimonies for the Church,* vol. 4, p. 414. (1880)

Continued Growth Important.—Men in responsible positions should improve continually. They must not anchor upon an old experience and feel that it is not necessary to become scientific workers.—*Testimonies for the Church,* vol. 4, p. 93. (1876)

Scientific Education Important.—I have written to him [W. C. White] in regard to the students, and have impressed upon him the necessity of expediency in the matter of gaining an education in any scientific lines. This has all been opened up to me for some time, and I have spoken to several concerning the necessity of waking up on this matter.—Letter 43, 1895.

MEN AND WOMEN
NEEDED IN VARIOUS MINISTRIES

Ministry of All Types Is Highest Work.—The highest of all work is the ministry in its various lines, and it should be kept before the youth that there is no work more blessed of God than that of the gospel minister.

Let not our young men be deterred from entering the ministry. There is danger that through glowing representations some will be drawn out of the path where God bids them walk. Some have been encouraged to take a course of study in medical lines who ought to be preparing themselves to enter the ministry. The Lord calls for more men to labor in His vineyard. The words were spoken, "Strengthen the outposts: have faithful sentinels in every part of the world." God calls for you, young men. He calls for whole armies of young men who are large-hearted and large-minded, and who have a deep love for Christ and the truth.—*General Conference Daily Bulletin,* March 2, 1899, p. 129 (*Counsels on Health,* p. 558).

Volunteers Needed to Do Evangelistic Work.—The Lord calls for volunteers who will take their stand firmly on His side and will pledge themselves to unite with Jesus of Nazareth in doing the work that needs to be done now, just now. The talents of God's people are to be employed in giving the last message of mercy to the world. The Lord calls upon those connected with our schools and sanitariums and publishing houses to teach the youth to do evangelistic work. Our time and money must not be so largely employed in establishing sanitariums, food factories, food stores, and restaurants that other lines of work shall be neglected. Young men and women who should be engaged in the ministry, in Bible work, and in the canvassing work should not be bound down to mechanical employment.— *Counsels to Parents, Teachers, and Students,* pp. 494, 495. (1913)

SELF-SUPPORTING MISSIONARIES

Self-supporting Workers Needed for Unentered Territories.—In many places self-supporting missionaries can work successfully. It was as a self-supporting missionary that the apostle Paul labored in spreading the knowledge of Christ throughout the world. While daily teaching the gospel in the great cities of Asia and

Europe, he wrought at the trade of a craftsman to sustain himself and his companions. . . .

Throughout the world, messengers of mercy are needed. There is a call for Christian families to go into communities that are in darkness and error, to go to foreign fields, to become acquainted with the needs of their fellow men, and to work for the cause of the Master. If such families would settle in the dark places of the earth, places where the people are enshrouded in spiritual gloom, and let the light of Christ's life shine out through them, what a noble work might be accomplished.—*The Ministry of Healing*, pp. 154-156. (1905)

God Accepts Even Limited Talents in Service for Others.—Are there not men and women in this congregation who have a work to do for the Master? Are there not those here who should go into new places and work as missionaries? We need missionaries at home; and we need missionaries who will go out into new fields, and see what they can do. Trade upon your one talent or two talents. Although your talents may be limited, God will accept them. Why bury them in the earth? Go to work, and do your best, and God will give you some fruit for your labor. Oh, I would rather come to the Master with garnered sheaves than to have treasures of gold and of silver. Give me souls as the fruit of my labor, and I will not ask for convenience or ease in this world. Are there not men and women here whom God will call to give an account for the ability He has lent them? There are souls for whom you are to work; there are youth with whom you are to plead. There is work to be done in the temperance line; and here you sit, from Sabbath to Sabbath, listening to the truth, while souls are perishing around you. Why not let the light which God has given you shine on the pathway of others? I beg you to consider this matter seriously.—*Review and Herald*, December 18, 1888.

SPIRIT OF SELF-SACRIFICE NEEDED

Work in Same Self-sacrificing Spirit as in Beginning.—Work is to be done in all parts of the vineyard. In the early days of the message a right beginning was made, but work has not developed as God desired it to develop. Too much has been centered in Battle Creek and Oakland, and in a few other places. Our brethren should never have built so largely in one place as they have in Battle Creek. In many fields very little has been done to establish memorials for God. This is wrong. Years ago very many of our workers and people had the spirit of self-denial and self-sacrifice. Success attended their efforts. The Lord has signified that His work should be carried forward in the same spirit in which it was begun. The world is to be warned. Field after field is still unworked. Shall we as a people, by our actions, our business arrangements, our attitude toward a world unsaved, bear a testimony altogether different from the testimony borne by us twenty or thirty years ago? Shall we give evidence of spiritual disease and a lack of wise planning? Upon us has shone great light in regard to the last days of this earth's history. The sight of the souls perishing in sin should arouse us to give the light of present truth to those now in darkness. God's messengers must be clothed with power. They must have for the truth a reverence that they do not now possess. The Lord's solemn, sacred message of warning must be proclaimed not merely in our churches, but in the most difficult fields and in the most sinful cities—in every place where the light of the third angel's message has not yet dawned. Every one is to hear the last call to the marriage supper of the Lamb.—Letter 128, 1902 (*The Kress Collection,* pp. 72, 73).

INFUSION OF THE HOLY SPIRIT

Holy Spirit Empowers Workers.—All who desire an opportunity for true ministry, and who will give themselves unreservedly to God, will find in the canvassing work opportunities to speak upon many things pertaining to the future, immortal life. The experience thus gained will be of the greatest value to those who are fitting themselves for the ministry. It is the accompaniment of the Holy Spirit of God that prepares workers, both men and women, to become pastors to the flock of God. As they cherish the thought that Christ is their Companion, a holy awe, a sacred joy, will be felt by them amid all their trying experiences and all their tests. They will learn how to pray as they work. They will be educated in patience, kindness, affability, and helpfulness. They will practice true Christian courtesy, bearing in mind that Christ, their Companion, cannot approve of harsh, unkind words or feelings. Their words will be purified. The power of speech will be regarded as a precious talent, lent them to do a high and holy work. The human agent will learn how to represent the divine Companion with whom he is associated. To that unseen Holy One he will show respect and reverence because he is wearing His yoke and is learning His pure, holy ways. Those who have faith in this divine Attendant will develop. They will be gifted with power to clothe the message of truth with a sacred beauty.—*Testimonies for the Church,* vol. 6, p. 322. (1900)

PREPARING MEDICAL MISSIONARIES

Qualified Ministers and Physicians Are Both Needed.— I am pleased that there are those who desire to be medical missionaries. But all cannot be medical missionaries in the whole sense in which it is now carried. There are those who must be qualified for the work to be done now in bringing the last message of warning to all cities and in all towns in all parts of our world. They cannot engage themselves for a stated number of years to learn the work of a medical missionary. While some feel that this is their work and choose to put themselves under training for this work, others feel that they must train themselves to be faithful ministers, skillful shepherds of the flock of God, that they may bring from the storehouse meat in due season for sheep and lambs.—Letter 86a, 1893 (*The Ellen G. White 1888 Materials,* p. 1148).

Missionary Nurses to Be Educated by Physicians.—In our schools missionary nurses should receive lessons from well-qualified physicians, and as a part of their education should learn how to battle with disease and to show the value of nature's remedies. This work is greatly needed. . . . God calls for reformers to stand in defense of the law which He has established to govern the physical system. They should at the same time maintain an elevated standard in the training of the mind and the culture of the heart, that the Great Physician may cooperate with the human helping hand in doing a work of mercy and necessity in the relief of suffering.—*Testimonies for the Church,* vol. 6, p. 136. (1900)

YOUTH TO BE TRAINED TO DO CITY WORK

Youth Are Most Able to Minister to People's Needs.— If the young men in our cities would unite their efforts to discountenance ungodliness and crime, their influence would greatly advance the cause of reform. It is the privilege and the duty of every youth, as an angel of mercy, to minister to the wants and woes of mankind. There is no class that can achieve greater results for God and humanity than the young.—*Signs of the Times,* November 3, 1881.

Youth to Be Taught to Be Useful Adults.—The true motive of service is to be kept before old and young. The students are to be taught in such a way that they will develop into useful men and women. Every means that will elevate and ennoble them is to be employed. They are to be taught to put their powers to the best use.—*Review and Herald,* May 26, 1904.

Youth to Be Blessing to Society.—Students at school should have had their moral sensibilities aroused to see and feel that society has claims upon them, and that they should live in obedience to natural law, so that they can, by their existence and influence, by precept and example, be an advantage and blessing to society. It should be impressed upon the youth that all have an influence that is constantly telling upon society, to improve and elevate, or to lower and debase.—*Counsels to Parents, Teachers, and Students,* p. 84. (1913)

Youth Will Have God's Help.—God will help our youth as He helped Daniel, if they will make the unreserved surrender of the will to Him that Daniel made, and will appreciate the opportunities of growing in understanding. He will give them wisdom and knowledge, and will fill their hearts with unselfishness. He will put into their minds plans of enlargement, and will inspire them with hope and courage as they seek to bring others under the sway of the Prince of peace.—Manuscript 38, 1904 (*Manuscript Releases,* vol. 4, p. 125).

Competent Leaders to Uphold High Ideals Before Young Workers.—More attention should be given to training and educating missionaries with a special reference to work in the cities. Each company of workers should be under the direction of a competent leader, and it should ever be kept before them that they are to be missionaries in the highest sense of the term. Such systematic labor, wisely conducted, would produce blessed results.

Something has been done in this line, but too frequently the work has dwindled down, and nothing permanent has been accomplished. There is need now of earnest labor. The young men who go forth in the employ of the General Conference are to understand that they are not merely to preach, but to minister, to act like men who are weighted with solemn responsibility to seek and to save that which is lost.—Letter 34, 1892 (*Medical Ministry,* p. 301).

Youth Learn From Working With Experienced Workers.—Many young men who have had the right kind of education at home are to be trained for service and encouraged to lift the standard of truth in new places by well-planned and faithful work. By associating with our ministers and experienced workers in city work, they will gain the best kind of training. Acting under divine guidance and sustained by the prayers of their more experienced fellow workers, they may do a good and blessed work. As they unite their labors with those of the older workers, using their youthful energies to the very best account, they will have the companionship of heavenly angels; and as workers together with God, it is their privilege to sing and pray and believe, and work with courage and freedom. The confidence and trust that the presence of heavenly agencies will bring to them and to their fellow workers will lead to prayer and praise and the simplicity of true faith.

There should be no delay in this well-planned effort to educate the church members. Persons should be chosen to labor in the large cities who are fully consecrated and who understand the sacredness and importance of the work. Do not send those who are not qualified in these respects. Men are needed who will push the triumphs of the cross, who will persevere under discouragements and privations, who will have the zeal and resolution and faith that are indispensable to the missionary field. And to those who do not engage personally in the work I would say: Do not hinder those who are willing to work, but give them encouragement and support.—*Testimonies for the Church,* vol. 9, p. 119. (1909)

Experienced Workers to Accompany Youthful Medical Missionaries.—There is a grand work to be done in relieving suffering humanity, and through the labors of students who are receiving an education and training to become efficient medical missionaries the people living in many cities may become acquainted with the truths of the third angel's message. Consecrated leaders and teachers of experience should go out with these young workers at first, giving them instruction how to labor. When favors of food are offered by those who fear and honor God, these favors may be accepted. Thus opportunity will be found for conversation, for explaining the Scriptures, for singing Bible songs and praying with the family. There are many to whom such labor as this would prove a blessing.—*Testimonies and Experiences Connected With the Loma Linda Sanitarium and College of Medical Evangelists* (Pamphlet 095), pp. 15, 16 (*Counsels on Health,* p. 542). (1906)

Married Couples to Supervise Young Workers.—There

should be connected with the mission married persons who will conduct themselves with the strictest propriety. . . .

Even though the men and women at the head of our missions are in character as pure as fine gold, they need constant connection with God in order to keep themselves pure and to know how to manage the youth discreetly, so that all shall keep their thoughts untainted, uncorrupted. Let the lessons be of an elevated, ennobling character, that the mind may be filled with pure and noble thoughts.—Manuscript 19a, 1890 (*General Conference Daily Bulletin,* February 6, 1893, p. 162).

Education of Young Workers to Be Thorough.—Wise, experienced teachers will be needed [to teach in the new college in Washington, D.C.]—men and women who can give the youth lessons in business lines, and who can teach them, also, how to do true missionary work. Nothing is to be neglected that will give a thorough training in right principles.—*Review and Herald,* May 26, 1904.

Frivolous Young Workers Denigrate Outreach Efforts.—The Lord has many precious souls in our large cities, who should be reached by the special truths for this time. But the course pursued by young men and young women connected with the mission is frivolous, degrading the work, and demoralizing the mission. Such defective characters separate God from the mission-rooms. It does not require weeks or months to read the character of many of the workers. Their conduct is an offense to God. There are wrongs existing in society which Christians will not practice, but abhor. Let those who are frivolous and carnally minded be placed in our missions, and their influence tends to lower everything connected with the mission.—*General Conference Daily Bulletin,* February 6, 1893, p. 162.

CITY EVANGELISM TRAINING SCHOOLS

Focus Needed on Preparing City Workers.—As a people, we are not doing one fiftieth of what we might do as active missionaries. If we were only vitalized by the Holy Spirit, there should be a hundred missionaries where there is now one. In every city there should be a corps of organized, well-disciplined workers; not merely one or two, but scores should be set to work. . . . More attention should be given to training and educating missionaries with special reference to work in cities.—*General Conference Daily Bulletin,* January 30, 1893, p. 37.

Homelike Setting Good for Training Missionary Workers.—Brother and Sister [Stephen and Hetty] Haskell have rented a house in one of the best parts of the city [Nashville], and have gathered round them a family of helpers, who day by day go out giving Bible readings, selling our papers, and doing medical missionary work. During the hour of worship, the workers relate their experiences. Bible studies are regularly conducted in the home, and the young men and young women connected with the mission receive a practical, thorough training in holding Bible readings and in selling our publications. The Lord has blessed their labors, a number have embraced the truth, and many others are deeply interested.

It was in this way that the fishermen who left their nets at the call of Christ were trained. A similar work should be done in many cities. The young people who go out to labor in these cities should be under the direction of experienced, consecrated leaders. Let the workers be provided with a good home, in which they may receive thorough training. The Lord has a precious, sacred work of soul-saving to be done in the world, and it is to be done now. This work is to be carried forward on a higher plane of individual responsibility than ever before.—*Review and Herald,* September 7, 1905.

Training to Include Personal Labor and Public Meetings.—Of equal importance with public effort is house-to-house work in the homes of the people. In large cities there are certain classes who cannot be reached by public meetings. These must be searched out as the shepherd searches for his lost sheep. Diligent personal effort must be put forth in their behalf. When personal work is neglected, many precious opportunities are lost, which, were they improved, would advance the work decidedly.

Again, as the result of the presentation of truth in large congregations, a spirit of inquiry is awakened, and it is especially important that this interest be followed by personal labor. Those who desire to investigate the truth need to be taught to study diligently the word of God. Someone must help them to build on a sure foundation. At this critical time in their religious experience, how important it is that wisely directed Bible workers come to their help, and open to their understanding the treasure-house of God's word!

A well-balanced work can be carried on best in the cities when a Bible school for the training of workers is in progress while public meetings are being held. Connected with this training school or city mission should be experienced laborers of deep spiritual understanding, who can give the Bible workers daily instruction, and who can also unite wholeheartedly in the general public effort. And as men and women are converted to the truth, those standing at the head of the mission should, with much prayer, show these new converts how to experience the power of the truth in their hearts. Such a mission, if conducted by those who know how to manage wisely, will be a light shining in a dark place.—*Gospel Workers,* pp. 364, 365. (1915)

EDUCATION CONTRACTS

Training to Be Coupled With Service Contract.—Before persons are admitted to our mission training schools, let there be a written agreement that after receiving their education they will give themselves to the work for a specified time. This is the only way that our missions can be made what they should be. Let those who connect themselves with the missions be straightforward, and take hold of the work in a businesslike manner. Those who are controlled by a sense of duty, who daily seek wisdom and help from God, will act intelligently, not from selfish motives, but from the love of Christ and the truth. Such will not hesitate to give themselves unreservedly, soul, body, and spirit, to the work. They will study, work, and pray for its advancement.—*General Conference Daily Bulletin,* February 6, 1893, pp. 162, 163.

CITY EVANGELISM EXPERIENCE NEEDED

Experience in City Evangelism Strengthens Faith.— Those who have crowded into Battle Creek and are being held there see and hear many things that tend to weaken their faith and engender unbelief. They would gain a more practical knowledge in an effort to impart to others that which they receive of the word of God. They should scatter out and be working in all our cities under the training of men who are sound in the faith. If those who teach these workers are true and loyal, a great work will be accomplished.

There is to be a working of our cities as they never have been worked. That which should have been done twenty, yea, more than twenty years ago, is now to be done speedily. The work will be more difficult to do now than it would have been years ago, but it will be done.

Our work is made exceedingly hard because of many false theories that have to be met, and because of the dearth of efficient teachers and willing helpers.—Letter 277, 1905 (*The Paulson Collection,* pp. 109, 110).

Refusal to Use Talents Eventually Renders Them Useless.—You may fold your hands saying, "I am only a lay member of the church; it is a hopeless task for me to undertake." But have you yoked up with Christ? Are you laboring in His way? Oh, let it no longer be a source of grief to the heavenly intelligences and to Him who has paid such an infinite price for souls, that you refuse to be channels of light, that you refuse to cooperate with the heavenly agencies for the salvation of souls! But let us "awake out of sleep," and put all our God-given abilities into the work, that it may be written in the books that we are "redeeming the time, because the days are evil." If we keep our talents inactive, we lose all ability to make use of them. The mind is a gift of God, designed to be improved and developed, that we may be able to enlighten others; but it may be perverted and misused in doing Satan's work.—*Review and Herald,* April 21, 1896.

THE AGED NOT TO BE
ASSIGNED TO WORK IN CITIES

City Ministry Not Advisable for Elderly or Feeble.— Feeble or aged men and women should not be sent to labor in unhealthful, crowded cities. Let them labor where their lives will not be needlessly sacrificed. Our brethren who bring the truth to the cities must not be obliged to imperil their health in the noise and bustle and confusion, if retired places can be secured.—Letter 168, 1909 (*Medical Ministry,* p. 309).

Chapter 7

TEACHING AND
REAPING METHODS

Church Members to Be Instructed How to Work for Others.—It is the duty of those who stand as leaders and teachers of the people to instruct church members how to labor in missionary lines and then to set in operation the great, grand work of proclaiming widely this message which must arouse every unworked city before the crisis shall come, when, through the working of satanic agencies, the doors now open to the message of the third angel shall be closed. God requires that we shall give the message of present truth to every city, and not keep the work bound up in a few places. Wherever an opening for the truth can be found, there let men be stationed who are capable of presenting its teachings with a power and conviction that will reach hearts.—Manuscript 61, 1909 (*Manuscript Releases,* vol. 10, pp. 215, 216).

Church Members to Learn to Impart Truth to Others.—The precious, saving truth has been repeated over and over again to our church members, while right in the cities where our churches are organized, there are souls perishing for the want of knowledge that the members of our churches could impart. Aggressive warfare is scarcely known. If believers were wide awake, were watching for opportunities to diffuse light, they would find plenty of work to do. The earnestness, the sobriety, the revelation of the sense of solemn responsibility which rests upon the followers of Christ, would count strongly in favor of the truth. Those who are self-sacrificing Christians will make an impression upon their neighbors by living a life of practical godliness. They will earnestly labor in the Master's service, showing forth the praises of Him who has called them out of darkness into His marvelous light. They will obey the instruction of Christ, "Let your light so shine before men, that they may see your good works, and glorify your Father which is in heaven." Every member of the church should learn how to communicate light to others who sit in darkness. Let every one watch for souls "as they that must give account."—*Review and Herald,* June 11, 1895.

PROCLAIM BIBLICAL TRUTH

Start by Presenting the Gospel as Clearly as Possible.— There is a sacred, solemn work to be done in lifting the standard high among those who have yet to hear the very first call to the gospel feast. Every kind of work is to come in its order. We are to lift the voice and proclaim the message upon the highways, and gather in all who will come to the marriage supper of the Lamb. This we are doing. We are placing our camp meetings in cities and towns where the message of present truth has not been heard. We do not at first proclaim to these souls doctrinal subjects of which they have no understanding. The very first and the most important thing is to melt and subdue the soul by presenting our Lord Jesus Christ as the sin-bearer, the sin-pardoning Saviour, making the gospel as clear as possible.—Letter 4, 1899.

Unveil Truths of God's Word to Those Who Will Listen.— In our towns and cities are souls living in ignorance of the truths of God's word; many are perishing in sin. Some out of curiosity come to our houses of worship. Let every discourse preached be a revelation of the great truths applicable to this time. Unveil the mysteries of redemption before the students in the school and before the congregations who assemble to hear the word. This is knowledge needed by the educated and the unlearned. The highest education will be found in studying the mystery of godliness. The great truths of God's word, if believed and received and carried into the life practice, will result in education of the highest order.— *Counsels to Parents, Teachers, and Students,* p. 398. (1913)

Bible Truth to Be Proclaimed in Simplicity So All Can Understand.—The Lord is speaking to His people at this time, saying, Gain an entrance into the cities, and proclaim the truth in simplicity and in faith. The Holy Spirit will work through your efforts to impress hearts. Introduce no strange doctrine into your message, but speak the simple words of the gospel of Christ, which young and old can understand. The unlearned as well as the educated are to comprehend the truths of the third angel's message, and they must be taught in simplicity. If you would approach the people acceptably, humble your hearts before God and learn His ways.—*Review and Herald,* January 18, 1912 (*Medical Ministry,* p. 299).

Unfold Bible Truth Only as Fast as It Is Understood.— Last night in my sleeping hours I seemed to be meeting with my brethren, listening to One who spoke as having authority. He said, "Many souls will attend this meeting who are honestly ignorant of the truths which will be presented before them. They will listen and become interested, because Christ is drawing them; conscience tells them that what they hear is true, for it has the Bible for its foundation. The greatest care is needed in dealing with these souls. . . . Do not at the outset press before the people the most objectionable features of our faith, lest you close the ears of those to whom these things come as a new revelation.

"Let such portions of truth be dealt out to them as they may be able to grasp and appreciate; though it should appear strange and startling, many will recognize with joy that new light is shed on the word of God; whereas if truth were presented in so large a measure that they could not receive it, some would go away, and never come again. More than this, they would misrepresent the truth; in their explanation of what was said, they would so wrest the Scriptures as to confuse other minds. We must take advantage of circumstances now. Present the truth as it is in Jesus. There must be no combative or controversial spirit in the advocacy of truth."—Manuscript 44, 1894 (*Special Testimonies to Ministers and Workers,* Series A, No. 3, pp. 13, 14).

TOPICS TO BE PREACHED

Many Know Only What Their Ministers Tell Them.—The people know nothing of the truth. They know nothing of the reasons of our faith. They believe what the church ministers tell them. Is there then to be no effort made that they shall know what the truth is for this time? What can be done in these cities, without money, to start the work? If you continually see places where you think you can use means to advantage, must these countries be left and the ground not plowed nor sown? Will the Lord be pleased with this kind of neglect?—Letter 9a, 1893 (*Manuscript Releases,* vol. 11, p. 7).

Preach Signs of Christ's Soon Return.—We feel that the time has come for decided efforts to be made in our cities. Read the twenty-first chapter of Luke. This is the message that we are to bear. It is a most solemn message for this time.—Letter 160, 1906.

Seventh-day Sabbath to Be Emphasized.—There are many places where the means should have been appropriated to make aggressive warfare in cities and towns in connection with tent efforts, and raise up churches which should be as memorials of truth and righteousness. Every stroke should tell for God and His holy Sabbath. That is to stand out in all our work distinctly and pronounced, to be a witness that the seventh day is the sign, the seal of God.—Letter 45, 1900 (*Manuscript Releases,* vol. 9, p. 88).

PUBLIC EVANGELISM IN THE LARGE CITIES

Rent Halls or Other Suitable Places for Public Meetings.—In places where the truth is not known, brethren who are adapted to the work might hire a hall, or some other suitable place to assemble, and gather together all who will come. Then let them instruct the people in the truth. They need not sermonize, but take the Bible, and let God speak directly out of His word. If there is only a small number present, they can read a "Thus saith the Lord," without a great parade or excitement; just read and explain the simple gospel truth, and sing and pray with them.—*Review and Herald,* September 29, 1891.

Evangelistic Endeavors to Include Follow-up.—In our efforts to reach the people, there is danger of adopting methods that will not produce the best results. Plans may be followed which seem to excite much interest for the time; but the effect proves that the work is not abiding. The use of the gospel wagon* may accomplish some good; but in most cases the after-results will be disappointing. People will be attracted by the music and will listen to the addresses and appeals that are made. But the workers pass rapidly from place to place, and there is not time for persons to become established in the faith. The impressions made are soon effaced. Little seed has been sown that springs up and bears fruit. When the season is ended, there will be few sheaves to be gathered. . . .

In many places it is next to impossible to find entrance to any house of worship. Prejudice, envy, jealousy are so strong that often we can find no place in which to speak to the people the word of life. If camp meetings can be held in different places, those who wish to hear can have the opportunity. Souls that are starving for the bread of life will be fed.

Instead of having mammoth camp meetings in a few localities, more good would often be done by having small meetings in many places. Let these be held in cities and towns where the message of present truth has not been presented. . . .

This should be followed up by a tent meeting and Bible work. Experienced laborers with their assistants should remain in the field to search out all who are interested. They should work as if searching for the lost sheep. Many who came to the camp meeting merely to hear or see some new thing will be impressed by the truth, and some will take their stand to obey. . . .

---

* A horse-drawn wagon decorated to attract attention and moved into a city to be used as a platform from which to present the message.

In these meetings we should not at first present doctrinal subjects, of which the hearers have no understanding. Hold the attention of the people by presenting the truth as it is in Jesus. The very first and most important thing is to melt and subdue the soul by presenting our Lord Jesus Christ as the sin-pardoning Saviour. Keep before the people the cross of Calvary. What caused the death of Christ? The transgression of the law. Show that Christ died to give men an opportunity to become loyal subjects of His kingdom.

Let the truth be presented, not in long, labored discourses, but in short talks, right to the point. Educate, educate, in regard to thorough, whole-souled service. Thorough consecration, much prayer, an intense earnestness, will make an impression; for angels of God will be present to move upon the hearts of the hearers.

Let there be singing and instrumental music. Musical instruments were used in religious services in ancient times. The worshipers praised God upon the harp and cymbal, and music should have its place in our services. It will add to the interest.—Manuscript 3, 1899 (*General Conference Daily Bulletin,* March 2, 1899, p. 128).

Open-air Meetings Effective in Some Places.—The cities must have more labor. There are places where the people can best be reached by open air meetings. There are many who can do this line of work, but they must be clad with the whole armor of righteousness. We are altogether too delicate in our work; yet propriety and sound sense are needed.—Manuscript 139, 1898 (*An Appeal for Missions* [Pamphlet 004], p. 15).

SPEAKERS AT CITY TENT MEETINGS

Best Possible Speakers to Be Used in City Camp Meetings.*—We all need to be wide awake, that, as the way opens, we may advance the work in the large cities. We are far behind in

---

* Used here to mean evangelistic meetings for members and nonmembers, almost always held in tents.

following the instruction to enter these cities and erect memorials for God. Step by step we are to lead souls into the full light of truth. We are to continue working until a church is organized and a humble house of worship built. . . .

In every city there is work to be done. Laborers are to go into our large cities and hold camp meetings. In these meetings, the very best talent is to be employed, that the truth may be proclaimed with power. Men of varied gifts are to be brought in. One man has not all the gifts required for the work. To make a camp meeting successful, several workers are needed. No one man should feel that it is his prerogative to do all the important work.—*Review and Herald,* September 30, 1902.

Speakers to Guard Their Words.—If in the camp meetings held in our cities the speakers are careful in all they say, hearts will be reached as the truth is proclaimed in the power of the Spirit. The love of Christ received into the heart will banish the love of error. The love and benevolence manifested in the life of Christ are to be manifested in the lives of those who work for Him. The earnest, untiring activity that marked His life is to mark their lives. The character of the Christian is to be a reproduction of the character of Christ. . . .

This line of work is not to be looked upon as separate and distinct from other lines of camp meeting work. Each line of God's work is closely related with every other line. And while the different lines are distinct, they are to advance in perfect harmony. . . .

Let all who can, give themselves to the long-neglected work in our cities, a work that has been looked at and then passed by on the other side, as the wounded man was passed by, by the priest and Levite. Take up the work in the cities, wholeheartedly, intelligently, unselfishly.—*Pacific Union Recorder,* October 23, 1902.

AVOID EXTRAVAGANT DISPLAY

Grand Display Not Needed.—I wish to speak decidedly. It

is not the plan of God for His church to arrange at any time to make a grand display in our cities on any occasion. The Lord is displeased and dishonored when His entrusted means is used in such displays. I was permitted to have the recent display presented to me, and I was instructed that the money used thus should have been used to relieve the situation of some who have lent means to our institutions and now need that means. There are those who lent their means in good faith, but who, though they have called and pleaded for their money, have not been able to obtain it. Means borrowed from our people is to be returned when called for.—Manuscript 162, 1905 (*Manuscript Releases,* vol. 10, p. 230).

Prayer and Holy Spirit Will Accomplish More Than Outward Display.—Those who do the work of the Lord in the cities must put forth calm, steady, devoted effort for the education of the people. While they are to labor earnestly to interest the hearers and to hold this interest, yet at the same time they must carefully guard against anything that borders on sensationalism. In this age of extravagance and outward show, when men think it is necessary to make a display in order to gain success, God's chosen messengers are to show the fallacy of spending means needlessly for effect. As they labor with simplicity, humility, and graceful dignity, avoiding everything of a theatrical nature, their work will make a lasting impression for good.

There is a necessity, it is true, for expending money judiciously in advertising the meetings and in carrying forward the work solidly. Yet the strength of every worker will be found to lie, not in these outward agencies, but in trustful dependence upon God, in earnest prayer to Him for help, in obedience to His Word. Much more prayer, much more Christlikeness, much more conformity to God's will, is to be brought into the Lord's work. Outward show and extravagant outlay of means will not accomplish the work to be done.

God's work is to be carried forward with power. We need the baptism of the Holy Spirit. We need to understand that God will add to the ranks of His people men of ability and influence who are to act their part in warning the world. All in the world are not lawless and sinful. God has many thousands who have not bowed the knee to Baal. There are God-fearing men and women in the fallen churches. If this were not so, we would not be given the message to bear: "Babylon the great is fallen, is fallen." "Come out of her, My people." Many of the honest in heart are gasping for a breath of life from heaven. They will recognize the gospel when it is brought to them in the beauty and simplicity with which it is presented in God's Word.—*Testimonies for the Church,* vol. 9, pp. 109-111. (1909)

Extravagant Display Contrary to Will of God.—God has looked upon the great display made by some who have labored in New York; but He does not harmonize with that way of preaching the gospel. The solemn message becomes mingled with a large amount of chaff, which makes upon minds an impression that is not in harmony with our work. The good news of saving grace is to be carried to every place; the warning must be given to the world; but economy must be practiced if we move in the spirit of which Christ has given us an example in His life service. He would have nothing of such an outlay to represent health reform in any place. . . .

All the grand displays that have been made in the medical missionary work, or in buildings, or in dress, or in any line of adornment are contrary to the will of God. Our work is to be carefully studied, and is to be in accordance with our Saviour's plan. He might have had armies of angels to display His true, princely character; but He laid all that aside and came to our world in the garb of humanity, to suffer with humanity all the temptations wherewith man is tempted. . . .

God calls upon Seventh-day Adventists to reveal to the world that we are preparing for the mansions that Christ has gone to prepare for those who will purify their souls by obeying the truth as it is in Jesus. Let every soul who will come after Christ deny himself, and take up his cross, and follow Him. Thus saith the great Teacher.—Letter 309, 1905 (*Review and Herald*, August 6, 1914).

PERSONAL EVANGELISM

Personal Witness More Effective Than Public Preaching.— By [your] being social and coming close to them [people we wish to reach], the current of their thoughts will be changed quicker than by the most able discourses. The presentation of Christ in the family, by the fireside, and in small gatherings in private houses is more successful in securing souls to Jesus than are sermons delivered in the open air to the moving throng, or even in halls or churches.—*Review and Herald,* December 8, 1885.

Preaching Augmented With House-to-House Efforts.— The cities are to be worked, not merely preached to; there must be house-to-house labor. After the warning has been given, after the truth has been presented from the Scriptures, many souls will be convicted. Then great carefulness is needed. The human agent cannot do the work of the Holy Spirit; we are only the channels through which the Lord works. Too often a spirit of self-sufficiency comes in, if a measure of success attends the efforts of the worker. But there must be no exaltation of self, nothing should be attributed to self; the work is the Lord's, and His precious name is to receive all the glory. Let self be hid in Jesus.—*Review and Herald,* October 14, 1902.

NEIGHBORHOOD OUTREACH

Begin in Your Own Neighborhood.—The Lord has presented before me the work that must be done in our cities. The believers in these cities can work for God in the neighborhood of their homes. They are to work quietly and in humility, carrying with them wherever they go the atmosphere of heaven. If they keep self out of sight, pointing always to Christ, the power of their influence will be felt on the side of truth.—*Review and Herald,* August 12, 1902.

Christians Living in Cities Are to Witness to Others.— I address Christians who live in our large cities: God has made you depositaries of truth, not that you may retain it, but that you may impart it to others. You should visit from house to house as faithful stewards of the grace of Christ. As you work, devise, and plan, new methods will continually present themselves to your mind, and by use the powers of your intellect will be increased. A lukewarm, slack performance of duty is an injury to the soul for whom Christ has died. If we would find the pearls buried in the debris of the cities, we should go forth ready to do the work required by the Master. Some may work quietly, creating an interest, while others speak in halls. It is true that Satan will scheme in every possible way so as to benumb the senses, blind the eyes, and close the ears of men against the truth; but notwithstanding this, go to work. Labor from house to house, not neglecting the poor, who are usually passed by. Christ said, "He hath anointed me to preach the gospel to the poor," and we are to go and do likewise.—*Review and Herald,* June 11, 1895.

Share With Friends.—We should feel it our special duty to work for those living in our neighborhood. Study how you can best help those who take no interest in religious things. As you visit your friends and neighbors, show an interest in their spiritual as well as in their temporal welfare. Speak to them of Christ as a sin-pardoning Saviour. Invite your neighbors to your home, and read with them from the precious Bible and from books that explain its truths. Invite them to unite with you in song and prayer. In these little gatherings, Christ Himself will be present, as He has promised, and hearts will be touched by His grace.

Church members should educate themselves to do this work. This is just as essential as to save the benighted souls in foreign countries. While some feel the burden for souls afar off, let the many who are at home feel the burden of precious souls who are around them, and work just as diligently for their salvation.—*The Ministry of Healing,* pp. 152, 153. (1905)

Reach People Where They Are.—To reach the people, wherever they are, and whatever their position or condition, and to help them in every way possible—this is true ministry. By such effort you may win hearts and open a door of access to perishing souls. . . .

It is of little use to try to reform others by attacking what we may regard as wrong habits. Such effort often results in more harm than good. In His talk with the Samaritan woman, instead of disparaging Jacob's well, Christ presented something better. . . . This is an illustration of the way in which we are to work. We must offer men something better than that which they possess, even the peace of Christ, which passeth all understanding.—*The Ministry of Healing,* pp. 156, 157. (1905)

ALL TO BE REACHED

Entire Human Family Is Our Congregation.—The love that was manifested in the life and character of Christ is no narrow, selfish affection. You are to be constrained by His love to preach the gospel in the regions beyond you, and not to boast in another man's line of things made ready to your hand. "But he that glorieth, let him glory in the Lord. For not he that commendeth himself is approved, but whom the Lord commendeth." The work ever before the minister of Christ is to preach the gospel, both to those that are nigh, and "in regions beyond." It involves self-denial, and necessitates cross-bearing. This kind of work, that will lead us continually to be faithful home missionaries and to press forward into new fields, must be carried on more and more as we near the close of earth's history. The gospel is not to be restricted to any time or confined to any place. The world is the field for the gospel minister, and the whole human family is his congregation. When he has finished giving a discourse, his work is only just entered upon; for the word of life is to be presented from house to house. The truth must be carried from city to city, from street to street, from family to family. Every method by which access may be gained to the homes of the people must be tried; for the messenger must become acquainted with the people. The truth must be carried from province to province, from kingdom to kingdom. The highways and byways must be thoroughly gleaned, and the message must spread from continent to continent, until the whole earth is belted with the gospel of our Lord Jesus Christ.

Ministers and missionaries must ever keep in view the "regions beyond." The Saviour has said of His people, "Ye are the light of the world." The truth is to be proclaimed; the light is to shine forth in clear, steady rays. Self-denial, self-sacrifice, whole-heartedness, must be put into the work; the light must shine forth until precious souls are brought to take their stand on the Lord's side. Then the worker is to press on into the "regions beyond," where souls are to be gathered and precious light shine amid the moral darkness that enshrouds the people. Thus must the truth be preached until the minds of those who sit in darkness as under the pall of death are enlightened, and elevated, and broadened. Every worker must stand at his post of duty, not only to preach, but to come close to souls, to become acquainted with them at their homes, as did Jesus, working unselfishly, devotedly, until the work is well bound off. When one company is raised up to carry light to the community, openings will be seen that invite the laborers into the "regions beyond." The workers for God will ever be pressing onward, ever depending upon the guidance of the Holy Spirit.—*Bible Echo,* May 21, 1894.

Everyone in Need Is My Neighbor.—Wherever there is human need and suffering, there is a field for missionary work. There are many unpromising subjects about us who are sacrificing the powers of their God-given manhood to pernicious habits. Shall we despise them? No; the Lord Jesus has purchased their souls at an infinite price, even by the shedding of His heart's blood. Are you who profess to be the children of God, Christians in the full acceptation of the term, or in your life-practice are you only counterfeits, pretenders? Do you ask, as did Cain, "Am I my brother's keeper?" Will the Lord say to any of us as He said to Cain, "What hast thou done? the voice of thy brother's blood crieth unto me from the ground"? Shall we fail to do our God-given work, and not to seek to save that which was lost? There are many who ask, as did the lawyer, "Who is my neighbor?" The answer comes down to us in the circumstances that happened near Jericho, when the priest and the Levite passed by on the other side, and left the poor bruised and wounded stranger to be taken care of by the good Samaritan. Every one who is in suffering need is our neighbor. Every straying son and daughter of Adam, who has been ensnared by the enemy of souls and bound in the slavery of wrong habits that blight the God-given manhood or womanhood, is my neighbor.—*Review and Herald,* November 12, 1895.

Entire World to Be Worked for God.—In great distress I awoke. I went to sleep again, and I seemed to be in a large gathering. One of authority was addressing the company, before whom was spread out a map of the world. He said that the map pictured God's vineyard, which must be cultivated. As light from heaven shone upon anyone, that one was to reflect the light to others. Lights were to be kindled in many places, and from these lights still other lights were to be kindled.

The words were repeated: "Ye are the salt of the earth: but if the salt have lost his savor, wherewith shall it be salted? It is thenceforth good for nothing, but to be cast out, and to be trodden under foot of men. Ye are the light of the world. A city that is set on a hill cannot be hid. Neither do men light a candle, and put it under a bushel, but on a candlestick; and it giveth light unto all that are in the house. Let your light so shine before men, that they may see your good works, and glorify your Father which is in heaven" (Matthew 5:13-16).

I saw jets of light shining from cities and villages, and from the high places and the low places of the earth. God's word was obeyed, and as a result there were memorials for Him in every city and village. His truth was proclaimed throughout the world.—*Testimonies for the Church,* vol. 9, pp. 28, 29. (1909)

Sunshine of the Sun of Righteousness to Be Spread to the Needy.—There is a work to be done by our churches that few have any idea of. "I was an hungered," Christ says, "and ye gave Me meat: I was thirsty, and ye gave Me drink: I was a stranger, and ye took Me in: naked, and ye clothed Me: I was sick, and ye visited Me: I was in prison, and ye came unto Me." We shall have to give of our means to support laborers in the harvest field, and we shall rejoice in the sheaves gathered in. But while this is right, there is a work, as yet untouched, that must be done. The mission of Christ was to heal the sick, encourage the hopeless, bind up the broken-hearted. This work of restoration is to be carried on among the needy, suffering ones of humanity. God calls not only for your benevolence, but your cheerful countenance, your hopeful words, the grasp of your hand. Relieve some of God's afflicted ones. Some are sick, and hope has departed. Bring back the sunlight to them. There are souls who have lost their courage; speak to them, pray for them. There are those who need the bread of life. Read to them from the Word of God. There is a soul sickness no balm can reach, no medicine heal. Pray for these, and bring them to Jesus Christ. And in all your work, Christ will be present to make impressions upon human hearts.

This is the kind of medical missionary work to be done. Bring the sunshine of the Sun of Righteousness into the room of the sick and suffering. Teach the inmates of the poor homes how to cook. "He shall feed his flock like a shepherd," with temporal and spiritual food.—Manuscript 105, 1898 (*A Call to Medical Evangelism and Health Education,* pp. 22, 23).

Welfare of All Woven Together.—There should be no monopolizing of what belongs, in a measure, to all, high and low, rich and poor, learned and unlearned. Not a ray of light must be under-valued, not a ray shut out, not a gleam unrecognized, or even acknowledged reluctantly. Let all act their part for truth and righteousness. The interests of the different classes of society are indissolubly united. We are all woven together in the great web of humanity, and we cannot, without loss, withdraw our sympathies from one another. It is impossible for a healthy influence to be maintained in the church when this common interest and sympathy does not exist.—*Gospel Workers,* p. 331. (1915)

Target Groups

THE UNREACHED

Many City Dwellers Ignorant of Christ's Soon Return.— There are those in all our cities who have not had the truth presented to them; who have not heard the warning message of the Lord's soon coming; who have not heard that the end of all things is at hand. Unless messengers go to them in the Spirit of Christ, how shall these people hear the gospel invitation? How shall they know that their sins may be forgiven through the mercy of a crucified and risen Saviour?—*Review and Herald,* July 2, 1895.

THE POOR

Poor Respond to the Gospel.—The Lord's people are mainly made up of the poor of this world, the common people. Not many wise, not many mighty, not many noble are called. God hath "chosen the poor of this world." "The poor have the gospel preached to them." The wealthy are called, in one sense; they are invited, but they do not accept the invitation. But in these wicked cities the Lord has many who are humble and yet trustful.— Manuscript 17, 1898 (*Evangelism,* p. 565).

All Called to Help the Needy.—Brethren and sisters, as this appeal in behalf of the needy comes to you, I hope that you will respond. Let every member take a lively interest in this good work. Do not let Jesus be disappointed in you. The Word of God abounds with instruction as to how we should treat the widow and fatherless, and the needy, suffering poor. If all would do the work of the Master, the widow's heart would sing for joy, and hungry little children would be fed, the destitute would be clothed, and those ready to perish would be revived.—Manuscript 26, 1891 (*Medical Missionary*, July 1891).

Every Case of Need to Be Noted.—It is God's purpose that the rich and the poor shall be closely bound together by the ties of sympathy and helpfulness. He bids us interest ourselves in every case of suffering and need that shall come to our knowledge.

Think it not lowering to your dignity to minister to suffering humanity.—*Testimonies for the Church*, vol. 6, p. 279. (1900)

Best Way to Reach Hearts.—By showing an interest in the wants of suffering humanity we can best reach hearts. The culture of the mind and heart is much more easily accomplished when we feel such tender sympathy in others that we scatter our benefits and privileges to relieve their necessities.—Letter 116, 1897 (*Welfare Ministry*, pp. 192, 193).

Personal Involvement Needed.—In trying to help the poor, the despised, the forsaken, do not work for them mounted on the stilts of your dignity and superiority, for in this way you will accomplish nothing. Become truly converted, and learn of Him who is meek and lowly in heart. We must set the Lord always before us. As servants of Christ keep saying, lest you forget it, "I am bought with a price."

God calls not only for your benevolence, but for your cheerful countenance, your hopeful words, the grasp of your hand. As you visit the Lord's afflicted ones, you will find some from whom hope has departed; bring back the sunshine to them. There are those who need the bread of life; read to them from the Word of God. Upon others there is a soul sickness that no earthly balm can reach or physician heal; pray for these, and bring them to Jesus.—*Testimonies for the Church,* vol. 6, p. 277. (1900)

Help Poor Who Can Be Benefited.—The Lord's poor subjects are to be helped in every case where it will be for their benefit. They are to be placed where they can help themselves. We have no question in regard to the cases of this class of poor. The best methods of helping them are to be carefully and prayerfully considered.

The Lord lays this responsibility upon every church. . . . God suffers His poor to be in the borders of every church. . . . They are not to pass by the Lord's poor but they are to deny themselves of luxuries . . . that they may make the suffering, needy ones comfortable.

After this they may reach still farther to help those who are not of the household of faith, if they are the proper subjects to be helped.—Manuscript 46, 1900 (*Manuscript Releases,* vol. 4, pp. 421, 422; see also *Testimonies for the Church*, vol. 1, pp. 272-274).

Employment Opportunities to Be Provided.—What can be done where poverty prevails and is to be contended with at every step? Certainly the work is difficult. The necessary reformation will never be made unless men and women are assisted by a power outside of themselves. It is God's purpose that the rich and the poor shall be closely bound together by the ties of sympathy and helpfulness. Those who have means, talents, and capabilities are to use these gifts in blessing their fellow men. . . .

Attention should be given to the establishment of various industries so that poor families can find employment. Carpenters, blacksmiths, and indeed everyone who understands some line of useful labor, should feel a responsibility to teach and help the ignorant and the unemployed.—*The Ministry of Healing,* pp. 193, 194. (1905)

God Is Robbed When Poor Not Helped.—Every extravagance should be cut out of our lives, for the time which we have to work is none too long. All around us we see suffering humanity. Families are in want of food; little ones are crying for bread. The houses of the poor lack proper furniture and bedding. Many live in mere hovels, which are almost destitute of all conveniences. The cry of the poor reaches to heaven. God sees; God hears. But many glorify themselves. While their fellow men are poor and hungry, suffering for want of food, they expend much on their tables, and eat far more than they require. What an account men will by and by have to render for their selfish use of God's money! Those who disregard the provision God has made for the poor will find that they have not only robbed their fellow men, but that in robbing them, they have robbed God, and have embezzled His goods.—Manuscript 60, 1896 (*Special Testimonies for Ministers and Workers,* Series A, No. 9, pp. 68, 69).

Generosity Toward Others Will Not Result in Personal Poverty.—"The poor," He [Jesus] says, "shall never cease out of the land: therefore I command thee, saying, Thou shalt open thine hand wide unto thy brother, to thy poor, and to thy needy, in thy land" (Deuteronomy 15:11). . . .

None need fear that their liberality would bring them to want. Obedience to God's commandments would surely result in prosperity. . . .

The plan of life that God gave to Israel was intended as an object lesson for all mankind. If these principles were carried out today, what a different place this world would be!—*The Ministry of Healing,* pp. 186-188. (1905)

THE AFFLUENT, EDUCATED, AND POWERFUL

Higher Classes in Society to Be Reached.—The gospel message is to be preached in every city; for this is in accordance with the example of Christ and His disciples. Medical missionaries are to seek patiently and earnestly to reach the higher classes. If this work is faithfully done, professional men will become trained evangelists.—Manuscript 33, 1901 (*Medical Ministry,* p. 241).

Work for Higher Classes Needs Our Best Capabilities.— We are to present the truth to those in the highways. This work has been neglected. We have a work to do for the higher classes, and this work needs all our capabilities. While we are in no case to neglect the poor and destitute, we have neither men nor money for the work among the very lowest classes. We point our workers to a higher grade. All reasons for this I cannot explain now.

The fields ripe for the harvest have been spread before me. We must work for the higher class of people. Then we shall have strength and ability with which to carry forward in the lines which God has pointed out.—Letter 164, 1901, p. 2 (*Manuscript Releases,* vol. 4, pp. 420, 421).

Methods for Sharing Gospel With All Classes Needed.—The gospel invitation is to be given to the rich and the poor, the high and the low, and we must devise means for carrying the truth into new places and to all classes of people. The Lord bids us, "Go out into the highways and hedges, and compel them to come in, that My house may be filled." He says, "Begin in the highways; thoroughly work the highways; prepare a company who in unity with you can go forth to do the very work that Christ did in seeking and saving the lost."—Manuscript 3, 1899 (*Medical Ministry,* p. 312).

People of Influence Not to Be Ignored.—This fallen world is in strange hands. Men rule for hire, and preach for hire. In all business transactions there is a strife for the supremacy. If Christ should walk through the streets of our cities today, few would have interest enough to follow Him. Those who act a part in the government of the world have no part with Christ, who has declared, "Without Me ye can do nothing." Can they be successful statesmen who have not learned the ways and methods of the Great Teacher? The men in high positions of trust should be educated in the school of Christ. Do not shun these influential men.—*Review and Herald*, August 21, 1900.

Wealthy Reached Through Bible-based Presentations.—

The servants of Christ should labor faithfully for the rich men in our cities, as well as for the poor and lowly. There are many wealthy men who are susceptible to the influences and impressions of the gospel message, and who, when the Bible, and the Bible alone, is presented to them as the expositor of Christian faith and practice, will be moved by the Spirit of God to open doors for the advancement of the gospel. They will reveal a living faith in the word of God and will use their entrusted means to prepare the way of the Lord, to make straight in the desert a highway for our God.— *Testimonies for the Church*, vol. 9, pp. 113, 114. (1909)

Holy Spirit Uses Government Officials to Protect God's Work.—

But so long as Jesus remains man's intercessor in the sanctuary above, the restraining influence of the Holy Spirit is felt by rulers and people. It still controls to some extent the laws of the land. Were it not for these laws, the condition of the world would be much worse than it now is. While many of our rulers are active agents of Satan, God also has His agents among the leading men of the nation. The enemy moves upon his servants to propose measures that would greatly impede the work of God; but statesmen who fear the Lord are influenced by holy angels to oppose such propositions with unanswerable arguments. Thus a few men will hold in check a powerful current of evil. The opposition of the enemies of truth will be restrained that the third angel's message may do its work. When the final warning shall be given, it will arrest the attention of these leading men through whom the Lord is now working, and some of them will accept it, and will stand with the people of God through the time of trouble.—*The Great Controversy*, pp. 610, 611. (1911)

SECULAR CAMPUSES

Youth to Practice Virtues Described by the Apostle Peter.—If our youth would take heed to and practice the rules laid down in this chapter [2 Peter 1], what an influence they would exert on the side of righteousness, whether they were at Ann Arbor [i.e., in a state university], or in our institutions, or in any place of responsibility.—Letter 43, 1895 (*Peter's Counsel to Parents,* p. 48).

THE SECULAR-MINDED

Satan Seeks to Divert Minds From Truth.—The unwarned multitudes are fast becoming the sport of the evil one. Satan is leading them into many forms of folly and self-pleasing. Many are seeking for that which is novel and startling; their minds are far from God and the truths of His Word. At this time, when the enemy is working as never before to engross the minds of men and women and turn them from the truth, we should be laboring with increasing activity in the highways and also in the byways. Diligently, interestedly, we are to proclaim the last message of mercy in the cities—the highways—and the work is not to end there, but is to extend into the surrounding settlements and in the country districts—into the byways and the hedges.

All classes are to be reached. As we labor, we shall meet with various nationalities. None are to be passed by, unwarned. The Lord Jesus was the gift of God to the entire world—not to the higher classes alone, and not to any one nationality to the exclusion of others. His saving grace encircles the whole world. Whosoever will may drink of the water of life freely.—Letter 4, 1911 (*The Upward Look,* p. 60).

Minds to Be Influenced for Christ.—As physicians unite with ministers in proclaiming the gospel in the great cities of the land, their combined labors will result in influencing many minds in favor of the truth for this time.

From the light that God has given me, I know that His cause today is in great need of the living representatives of Bible truth. The ordained ministers alone are not equal to the task. God is calling not only upon the ministers, but also upon physicians, nurses, canvassers, Bible workers, and other consecrated laymen of varied talent who have a knowledge of present truth, to consider the needs of the unwarned cities. There should be one hundred believers actively engaged in personal missionary work where now there is but one. Time is rapidly passing. There is much work to be done before satanic opposition shall close up the way. Every agency must be set in operation, that present opportunities may be wisely improved.—*Review and Herald*, April 7, 1910 (*Medical Ministry*, pp. 248, 249).

VISITORS TO FAIRS AND CONVENTIONS

Fairs and Other Large Gatherings Provide Outreach Opportunities.—I was given instruction that as we approach the end, there will be large gatherings in our cities, as there has recently been in St. Louis,[*] and that preparations must be made to present the truth at these gatherings. When Christ was upon this earth, He took advantage of such opportunities. Wherever a large number of people was gathered for any purpose, His voice was heard, clear and distinct, giving His message. And as a result, after His crucifixion and ascension, thousands were converted in a day. The seed sown by Christ sank deep into hearts, and germinated, and when the disciples received the gift of the Holy Spirit, the harvest was gathered in.

The disciples went forth and preached the word everywhere with such power that fear fell upon their opposers, and they dared not do that which they would have done had not the evidence been so plain that God was working.

At every large gathering some of our ministers should be in at-

---

[*] World's Fair in St. Louis, Missouri, 1904.

tendance. They should work wisely to obtain a hearing and to get the light of the truth before as many as possible. . . .

We should improve every such opportunity as that presented by the St. Louis Fair. At all such gatherings there should be present men whom God can use. Leaflets containing the light of present truth should be scattered among the people like the leaves of autumn. To many who attend these gatherings these leaflets would be as the leaves of the tree of life, which are for the healing of the nations.

I send you this, my brethren [A. G. Daniells and W. W. Prescott], that you may give it to others. Those who go forth to proclaim the truth shall be blessed by Him who has given them the burden of proclaiming this truth. . . .

The time has come when, as never before, Seventh-day Adventists are to arise and shine, because their light has come, and the glory of the Lord has risen upon them.—Letter 296, 1904 (*Evangelism,* pp. 35, 36).

NOT ALL CALLED TO WORK EXCLUSIVELY FOR LOWEST CLASSES

Work for Both Poor and Rich Needed.—[*NOTE BY DR. DANIEL H. KRESS: "Before graduating from the University of Michigan, during the last year I spent three months in the city of Chicago, where we opened up a medical mission and aimed to help the outcasts and neglected, known as the down-and-outs, in the worst part of the city of Chicago. I enjoyed this work, and in my perplexity I thought possibly I should take up that work again. I wrote Sister White telling her of what I had been thinking, and in reply she said,"*]

In your letter you speak of the rescue work in the poorer parts of the city. I am glad that you feel a burden to help the very ones that need help. Christ desires His work to become the light of the world. He Himself came to make known to all classes the gospel of salvation. There may be associated with you some who should work among the unfortunate and the degraded, but you are especially fitted to labor for the higher classes. Your influence with them would be lessened should you be associated largely with the rescue work for those who are generally regarded as outcasts.—*The Kress Collection,* pp. 168, 169. Ellen White's response is from letter 158, 1909 (*Manuscript Releases,* vol. 7, pp. 329, 330).

Priorities Needed When Working for Lowest Classes.—The great question of our duty to humanity is a serious one, and much of the grace of God is needed in deciding how to work so as to accomplish the greatest amount of good. Not all are called to begin their work by laboring among the lowest classes. God does not require His workmen to obtain their education and training in order to devote themselves exclusively to these classes.—Manuscript 3, 1899 (*Evangelism,* p. 548).

Work for Lowest Classes Not to Supersede Worldwide Proclamation of Gospel.—We do not advise our people to open up a work in our cities, to the extent of erecting buildings to which they can invite the most depraved class of people to come and receive food and beds and treatment without money and without price. None are required to establish a work in any city which gives to an indiscriminate class an invitation to be supported by the charities of the Seventh-day Adventist people, whose special work is to bear an unpopular message to the world. The commission is given to bear the message to all nations.—Letter 90, 1900 (*Manuscript Releases,* vol. 4, p. 420).

Do Not Forbid Those Who Feel Called to Help Worst Parts of Cities.—If men feel that God has called them to devote all their missionary efforts to the worst part of the cities, no one should forbid them to work.—Letter 3, 1900 (*Manuscript Releases,* vol. 4, p. 421).

Obtain Financial Support From World to Fund Work for Most Degraded in Society.—If there are men who will take up the work of laboring for the most degraded, men upon whom God has laid the burden to labor for the masses in a variety of ways, let these converted ones go forth and gather from the world the means required to do this work. Let them not depend on the means which God intends shall sustain the work of the gospel.— Letter 205, 1899 (*Manuscript Releases,* vol. 20, p. 252).

Chapter 8

WORKING INSIDE
AND OUTSIDE CITIES

Some Must Live in Cities to Work for Others.—It is Satan's purpose to attract men and women to the cities, and to gain this object he invents every kind of novelty and amusement, every kind of excitement. And the cities of the earth today are becoming as were the cities before the Flood.

We should carry a continual burden as we see the fulfillment of the words of Christ. "As the days of Noe were, so shall also the coming of the Son of man be" (Matthew 24:37). In the days before the Flood, every kind of amusement was invented to lead men and women to forgetfulness and sin. Today, in 1908, Satan is working with intensity, that the same conditions of evil shall prevail. And the earth is becoming corrupt. Religious liberty will be little respected by professing Christians, for many of them have no understanding of spiritual things.

We cannot fail to see that the end of the world is soon to come. Satan is working upon the minds of men and women, and many seem filled with a desire for amusement and excitement. As it was in the days of Noah, every kind of evil is on the increase. Divorce and marriage is the order of the time. At such a time as this, the people who are seeking to keep the commandments of God should look for retired places away from the cities. Some must remain in the cities to give the last note of warning, but this will become more and more dangerous to do. Yet the truth for today must come to the world—truth as spoken by the lips of Him who understood the end from the beginning.—Manuscript 85, 1908 (*Manuscript Releases,* vol. 10, pp. 261, 262).

Lay Members Will Move to Cities to Conduct Evangelistic Work.—Close around us are cities and towns in which no efforts are made to save souls. Why should not families who know the present truth settle in these cities and villages, to set up there the standard of Christ, working in humility, not in their own way, but in God's way, to bring the light before those who have no knowledge of it? . . . There will be laymen who will move into towns and cities, and into apparently out-of-the-way places, that they may let the light which God has given them shine forth to others. Some whom they meet will not appear to be the most promising subjects, but the only question should be, Will they come into harmony with Christ? Will they become partakers of His spirit, so that their influence, in precept and example, will present the attractions of the Author of truth and righteousness?— *Review and Herald,* September 29, 1891 (*Christian Service,* p. 180).

Institutions to Be Located Outside Cities; Churches to Be Established Inside.—Repeatedly the Lord has instructed us that we are to work the cities from outpost centers. In these cities we are to have houses of worship, as memorials for God; but institutions for the publication of our literature, for the healing of the sick, and for the training of workers are to be established outside the cities. Especially is it important that our youth be shielded from the temptations of city life.

It is in harmony with this instruction that meetinghouses have been purchased and rededicated in Washington, D.C., and in Nashville, while the publishing houses and the sanitariums at these centers have been established away from the congested heart of the cities, as outpost centers. This is the plan that has been followed in the removal of other publishing houses and sanitariums into the country, and that is now being followed in Great Britain with regard to the London publishing house and also the training school there. We are now given opportunity to advance in the opening providences of God by helping our brethren in these and many other important centers to establish the work on a firm basis, in order that it may be carried forward solidly.—*Special Testimonies,* Series B, No. 8, pp. 7, 8. (1907)

CHURCHES

Churches to Be Established in Cities.—In every city where the truth is proclaimed, churches are to be raised up. In some large cities there must be churches in various parts of the city. In some places, meetinghouses will be offered for sale at reasonable rates, which can be purchased advantageously.—Letter 168, 1909 (*Medical Ministry,* p. 309). (For additional information, see chapter 10, "Planting Churches in the Cities.")

CITY MISSIONS*

Every City Should Have a City Mission.—Although a few places have been entered, many centers should be established where there would be employed hundreds of workers. In every city there should be a city mission that would be a training school for workers. Many of our brethren must stand condemned in the sight of God because they have not done the very work that God would have them do.—Letter 56, 1910 (portion in *Medical Ministry,* p. 303).

Samaritan Work to Serve Those Whom Society Ignores.— Nothing will or ever can give character to the work in the presentation of truth as that of helping the people just where they are, as this Samaritan work. A work properly conducted to save poor sinners that have been passed by the churches will be the entering wedge where the truth will find standing room. A different order of things needs to be established among us as a people, and in doing

---

* City missions were established in cities in the late nineteenth century to house and train workers, supply books for distribution, provide a place for public meetings, and offer health and social services.

this class of work there would be created an entirely different atmosphere surrounding the soul of the workers, for the Holy Spirit communicates to all those who are doing God's service, and those who are worked by the Holy Spirit will be a power for good in lifting up, strengthening, and saving the souls that are ready to perish.—Manuscript 14a, 1897 (*Evangelism,* pp. 567, 568).

City Mission Will Increase Other Calls for Help.—We have a large territory to work in our cities. When a mission is established in a city, calls for laborers will come from the surrounding country. According to the light given me, during the last thirty years not a thousandth part has been done of what ought to have been done. Plans for aggressive work should have been set in operation.—Letter 176, 1901.

EDUCATIONAL INSTITUTIONS

Church Schools to Be Established in Cities.—Much more can be done to save and educate the children of those who at present cannot get away from the cities. This is a matter worthy of our best efforts. Church schools are to be established for the children in the cities, and in connection with these schools provision is to be made for the teaching of higher studies where these are called for. These schools can be managed in such a way, part joining to part, that they will be a complete whole.—Manuscript 129, 1903 (*Manuscript Releases,* vol. 10, p. 258).

Parents Encouraged to Send Children to Church Schools.—The church has a special work to do in educating and training its children that they may not, in attending school or in any other association, be influenced by those of corrupt habits. The world is full of iniquity and disregard of the requirements of God. The cities have become as Sodom, and our children are daily exposed to many evils. Those who attend the public schools often associate with others more neglected than they, those who, aside from the time spent in the schoolroom, are left to obtain a street education. The hearts of the young are easily impressed; and unless their surroundings are of the right character, Satan will use these neglected children to influence those who are more carefully trained. Thus, before Sabbathkeeping parents know what is being done, the lessons of depravity are learned, and the souls of their little ones are corrupted.—*Counsels to Parents, Teachers, and Students,* p. 173. (1913)

Educating Students in the Country* Important to Saving Their Souls.—Let parents understand that the training of their children is an important work in the saving of souls. In country places abundant, useful exercise will be found in doing those things that need to be done, and which will give physical health by developing nerve and muscle. "Out of the cities" is my message for the education of our children.—Manuscript 85, 1908 (*Selected Messages,* book 2, p. 355).

SANITARIUMS†

Sanitariums to Reach All Classes.—Great light has been shining upon us, but how little of this light we reflect to the world! Heavenly angels are waiting for human beings to cooperate with them in the practical carrying out of the principles of truth. It is through the agency of our sanitariums and kindred enterprises that much of this work is to be done. These institutions are to be God's memorials, where His healing power can reach all classes, high and low, rich and poor. Every dollar invested in them for Christ's sake will bring blessings both to the giver and to suffering humanity.—*Testimonies for the Church,* vol. 7, pp. 58, 59. (1902)

---

* In her counsels, Ellen White distinguished between church schools established in cities and boarding schools established in the country.

† During Ellen White's lifetime, sanitariums were not like today's hospitals. They strongly emphasized health education, and patients often remained for weeks while regaining their health.

Sanitariums and Schools* Not to Be Established in Cities.—Some things have been presented to me that I deem of great importance. Light has been given that our institutions are not to be established in the midst of the cities. So great is the wickedness of these cities that much of what the eyes see and the ears hear has a demoralizing influence. Especially should our schools and sanitariums be located outside of the cities, in places where land can be secured. . . .

It would be a mistake for us to purchase or erect large buildings in the cities of southern California for sanitarium work, and those who see advantages in doing this are not moving understandingly. A great work is to be done in preparing these cities to hear the gospel message, but this work is not to be done by fitting up in them large buildings for the carrying forward of some wonderful enterprise.—Manuscript 114, 1902 (*Manuscript Releases,* vol. 10, pp. 209-211).

Best if Sanitariums Located in the Country.— Institutions for the care of the sick would be far more successful if they could be established away from the cities. And so far as possible, all who are seeking to recover health should place themselves amid country surroundings where they can have the benefit of outdoor life. Nature is God's physician. The pure air, the glad sunshine, the flowers and trees, the orchards and vineyards, and outdoor exercise amid these surroundings, are health-giving, life-giving.—*The Ministry of Healing,* pp. 263, 264. (1905)

City Crime Increases Need to Establish Sanitariums in Mountains.—As we draw near to the close of time the cities will become more and more corrupt, and more and more objectionable as places for establishing centers of our work. The dangers of travel will increase; confusion and drunkenness will abound. If there can be found places in retired mountain regions where it would be dif-

---

* Boarding schools.

ficult for the evils of the cities to enter, let our people secure such places for our sanitariums and advanced schools.—Manuscript 85, 1908 (*Manuscript Releases,* vol. 10, p. 260).

Sanitarium Buildings to Promote Health and Happiness, Not Extravagance.—As did Enoch, we must work in the cities but not dwell in them. Nothing that savors of extravagance is to be seen in the outlay of means for building or for furnishing because we have a prospect of receiving donations. Find a location that has a favorable atmosphere and carry on your work, but keep away from the residences of the rulers of the land. Exert your God-given powers for the people who need to be uplifted. Place not your institutions in the midst of the homes of wealthy men. If possible we must secure for the sanitarium a site that will not be crowded, where there is ground that can be cultivated. Nothing is to be done for display. By strict economy we are to show that we realize that we are strangers and pilgrims on the earth. . . .

In erecting our buildings we must keep away from the great men of the world, and then let them seek the help they need by moving away from their associates into more retired localities. Let their attention be drawn to a people who love and fear God. If the sanitarium is not near the houses of rich men, they will not have opportunity to comment unfavorably upon it because it is understood to be a place which receives suffering humanity of all classes. . . .

What is needed to give success? A large, expensive building? If so, we cannot have success. But this does not give success. It is the atmosphere of grace which surrounds the soul of the believer, the Holy Spirit working upon mind and heart, which makes him a savor of life unto life and enables God to bless his work. God would bind His family of workers together by common sympathy, pure affection. Love and respect for one another has a telling influence and is a representation of practical godliness. Unbelief is cold and repulsive, dark and forbidding, and can only deny and destroy, while the work of faith under all circumstances can lift the head in conscious dignity and firm trust in God. Even youthful hearts may reveal surpassing beauty and glory in the path of self-denial and self-sacrifice by following where Christ leads the way, lifting His cross and bearing it after Him to His Father's home in heaven, walking in the path cast up for the ransomed of the Lord. . . .

Let all our buildings be prepared for health and happiness, being so arranged that every unnecessary step shall be saved. Let the sanitarium be so located that the patients will have the benefits of sunlight. There should be a fireplace in every sleeping room where patients live. These inside arrangements must be made even though the building is not in an exact line with roads or other buildings. The rooms should be furnished with comfortable chairs not all made after the same pattern. The results will be far more satisfactory if the precision of the furniture is broken up. God has given us a plan for this in the variety of form and color seen in the things of nature. Means must be expended to obtain comfortable, restful articles of furniture. Patients will be much better pleased with them than if the furniture were all precisely the same.—Manuscript 85, 1899 (*Manuscript Releases,* vol. 10, pp. 241-247).

Properties Suitable for Sanitariums Should Be Considered.—In some important places there will be offered for sale properties that are especially suitable for sanitarium work. The advantages of these should be carefully considered.

In order that some of these places may be secured for our work, it will be necessary carefully to husband the resources, no extravagant outlay being made in any one place. The very simplicity of the buildings that we use will be a lesson in harmony with the truths we have to present. For our sanitarium work we must secure buildings whose appearance and arrangement will be a demonstration of health principles.—Letter 168, 1909 (*Medical Ministry,* p. 309).

Approval Withheld to Build Sanitarium in City.—With the light that I have had in regard to sanitariums where the sick are to be treated, I cannot give one word of counsel about huddling in the city. I cannot do it myself, and yet it may look very different to others. But with the light that I have, I could not advise placing a building in the city. You [F. B. Moran] are out of the city, I know. You are out at one side. That changes the proposition somewhat, but further than that, I could not say. I could not give you any advice. You will have to arrange that among yourselves because I could not give advice to build a sanitarium in any city. I could not do it, because it has been so distinctly laid before me that when a sanitarium is built it must be located where it can accomplish the end in view—the object for which it is established.—Manuscript 173, 1902 (*Manuscript Releases,* vol. 10, p. 250).

VEGETARIAN RESTAURANTS

Vegetarian Restaurants to Be Established in Cities.— God would have restaurants established in the cities. If properly managed, these will become missionary centers. In these restaurants publications should be kept at hand, ready to present to those who patronize the restaurant.

The question often arises, Should these restaurants be kept open on the Sabbath? The answer is, "No, no." The Sabbath is our mark and sign, and should not become obliterated. I have recently had special light upon this subject. Efforts will be made to keep the restaurants open on Sabbath, but this should not be done.— Manuscript 30, 1903 (*Sermons and Talks,* vol. 2, p. 226).

Vegetarian Restaurants to Teach Principles of Right Living.—Our restaurants must be in the cities; for otherwise the workers in these restaurants could not reach the people and teach them the principles of right living. And for the present we shall have to occupy meetinghouses in the cities. But erelong there will be such strife and confusion in the cities that those who wish to leave them will not be able. We must be preparing for these issues.—*General Conference Bulletin,* April 6, 1903, p. 88; *Review and Herald,* April 14, 1903 (*Selected Messages,* book 2, p. 142).

Spiritual Food to Be Shared by Workers at Restaurants.— The workers in our restaurants are to prepare for the future immortal life. Let them acquire the power and tact to prepare spiritual food for the souls of men and women in these large cities. Watch for souls as they that must give an account. The cities are to be warned, and these young men and young women should remember that time is precious. The world is increasing in wickedness as in the days of Noah.—Letter 279, 1905 (*A Call to Medical Evangelism and Health Education,* p. 22).

Cooking Classes to Be Conducted.—Every hygienic restaurant should be a school. The workers connected with it should be constantly studying and experimenting, that they may make improvement in the preparation of healthful foods. In the cities this work of instruction may be carried forward on a much larger scale than in smaller places. But in every place where there is a church, instruction should be given in regard to the preparation of simple, healthful foods for the use of those who wish to live in accordance with the principles of health reform. And the church members should impart to the people of their neighborhood the light they receive on this subject.—*Testimonies for the Church,* vol. 7, pp. 112, 113. (1902)

First-class Restaurants Will Result in Inquiries.—I have been instructed that one of the principal reasons why hygienic restaurants and treatment rooms should be established in the centers of large cities is that by this means the attention of leading men will be called to the third angel's message. Noticing that these restaurants are conducted in a way altogether different from the way in which ordinary restaurants are conducted, men of intelligence will begin to inquire into the reasons for the difference in business methods, and will investigate the principles that lead us to serve superior food. Thus they will be led to a knowledge of the message for this time.—*Testimonies for the Church,* vol. 7, pp. 122, 123. (1902)

Free Spiritual Literature to Be Provided.—Those who come to our restaurants should be supplied with reading matter. Their attention should be called to our literature on temperance and dietetic reform, and leaflets treating on the lessons of Christ should also be given them. The burden of supplying this reading matter should be shared by all our people. All who come should be given something to read. It may be that many will leave the tract unread, but some among those in whose hands you place it may be searching for light. They will read and study what you give them, and then pass it on to others.—*Testimonies for the Church,* vol. 7, p. 116. (1902)

Restaurants for Nonmembers to Be Operated at Camp Meetings.—At our camp meetings* there should be a restaurant where the poor can obtain wholesome, well-prepared food as cheaply as possible. There should also be another restaurant in which food is especially prepared for the education of outsiders, where they may see a representation of health-reform diet.—*Pacific Union Recorder,* October 23, 1902.

TREATMENT ROOMS

Treatment Rooms and Vegetarian Restaurants to Be Associated Together.—I have been given light that in many cities it is advisable for a restaurant to be connected with treatment rooms. The two can cooperate in upholding right principles. In connection with these it is sometimes advisable to have rooms that will serve as lodgings for the sick. These establishments will serve as feeders to the sanitariums located in the country.—*Testimonies for the Church,* vol. 7, p. 60. (1902)

---

* Revival meetings, often also evangelistic in nature, for members and nonmembers, held in a tent.

Chapter 9

CHRIST-CENTERED HEALTH MINISTRY*

THE LEADING EDGE

Health Ministry to Be Starting Point.—Medical missionary work has been presented as the entering wedge of present truth. It is by this work that hearts are reached, and those once prejudiced are softened and subdued. This is the work that is to be done today.—Letter 110, 1902 (*Manuscript Releases,* vol. 4, p. 374).

Health Evangelism Opens Doors for Sharing the Gospel.—The evangelization of the world is the work that God has given to those who go forth in His name. They are to be colaborers with Christ, revealing to those ready to perish His tender, pitying love. God calls for thousands to work for Him, not by preaching to those who know the truth, going over and over the same ground, but by warning those who have never heard the last message of mercy. Work, with a heart filled with an earnest longing for souls. Do medical missionary work. Thus you will gain access to the hearts of the people. The way will be prepared for more decided proclamation of the truth. You will find that relieving their physical suffering gives an opportunity to minister to their spiritual needs.

The Lord will give you success in this work, for the gospel is the power of God unto salvation when it is interwoven with the practical life, when it is lived and practiced. The union of Christlike work for the body and Christlike work for the soul is the true in-

---

* In Ellen White's time this was generally called medical missionary work.

terpretation of the gospel.—*A Call to Medical Evangelism and Health Education,* p. 7.

All in Need to Be Helped by Health Evangelism.—He [the Lord] sees in our cities many who have been blessed with a large share of mental and physical capabilities swept into the whirlpool of temptation. They must be reached. This is where health reform has been made the entering wedge. By this work many have been reached that would not otherwise have been reached. Men and women of strong, noble sentiments and deep sympathies have been aroused to do something, while priest and Levite have passed by on the other side. . . .

There is a work to be done in the cities of America that is very different from the work that has been done. . . . Not only are those who are in respectable grades of society to be worked for, [but] the fallen and degraded are to be gathered in. It is in the highways and hedges that souls will be found who need to be saved. Many are mentally blind, mentally wounded. There are those who have had educational privileges, who have valuable, receptive faculties, who have yielded to temptation. These are to be sought out. Some are in possession of more than ordinary talents, but they are dead in trespasses and sins, and they must be labored for.—Manuscript 33, 1899.

Christian Help Work to Bless Others.—You [Dr. J. H. Kellogg] speak of the work that is being done in Chicago. I am in full sympathy with the work that is being done there. I believe in helping along every line in which it is possible to help, following the steps of Christ. Those who take hold of this Christian help work who will consecrate themselves to God will find that He will be a present help to them in every hour of need. I know that the Lord will use those who will submit themselves to Him, and through the power of the Holy Spirit, they will be enabled to do the work that needs to be done.—Letter 43, 1895 (*Manuscript Releases,* vol. 4, p. 131).

Health Ministry Prepares Way for Reception of Truth.— The right hand is used to open doors through which the body may find entrance. This is the part the medical missionary work is to act. It is to largely prepare the way for the reception of the truth for this time. A body without hands is useless. In giving honor to the body, honor must also be given to the helping hands, which are agencies of such importance that without them the body can do nothing. Therefore the body which treats indifferently the right hand, refusing its aid, is able to accomplish nothing.—Manuscript 55, 1901 (*Medical Ministry,* p. 238).

Health Evangelism Work Necessary to Advance God's Work.— Medical missionary work is the right hand of the gospel. It is necessary to the advancement of the cause of God. As through it men and women are led to see the importance of right habits of living, the saving power of the truth will be made known. Every city is to be entered by workers trained to do medical missionary work. As the right hand of the third angel's message, God's methods of treating disease will open doors for the entrance of present truth.—*Testimonies for the Church,* vol. 7, p. 59. (1902)

Diseased Souls to Be Reached Through Health Evangelism.— I can see in the Lord's providence that the medical missionary work is to be a great entering wedge, whereby the diseased soul may be reached.—Letter 36, 1893 (*Counsels on Health,* p. 535).

World Open to Health Evangelism.— Medical missionary work brings to humanity the gospel of release from suffering. It is the pioneer work of the gospel. It is the gospel practiced, the compassion of Christ revealed. Of this work there is great need, and the world is open for it. God grant that the importance of medical missionary work shall be understood, and that new fields may be immediately entered.—Manuscript 55, 1901 (*Medical Ministry,* p. 239).

CHURCHES TO BE INVOLVED

Wherever Churches Are Established, Health Ministry Work to Be Started.—The question has been asked, did you not give Dr. [J. H.] Kellogg encouragement after he had entered into this work? I answer, I did; for I had been instructed that a work of this character should be done by all our churches; that a deep interest should be taken in this very line of work; that according to the light which the Lord had been pleased to give me, this line of work should have been taken hold of with resolution by our ministers, not to create a large center in one place, but to establish the work in many cities and to arouse the people to give of the Lord's money for the work in behalf of suffering humanity.

The Lord gave me light that in every place where a church was established, medical missionary work was to be done. But there was in the Battle Creek church a great deal of selfishness. Those at the very heart of the work indulged their own wishes in a way that dishonored God. Dr. Kellogg was not sustained in the health reform work, the importance of which had been kept before the church for thirty years. This work was hindered because of the feelings and prejudices of some in Battle Creek who were not disposed to conform their course of action to the Word of God regarding health reform principles.—Manuscript 175, 1898 (*Battle Creek Letters,* p. 11).

Every Church Is to Serve Those in Need.—The work of gathering in the needy, the oppressed, the suffering, the destitute, is the very work which every church that believes the truth for this time should long since have been doing. We are to show the tender sympathy of the Samaritan . . . , feeding the hungry, bringing the poor that are cast out to our homes, gathering from God every day grace and strength that will enable us to reach to the very depths of human misery and help those who cannot possibly help themselves. In doing this work we have a favorable opportunity to set forth Christ the Crucified One.—*Testimonies for the Church,* vol. 6, p. 276. (1900)

Wisdom Needed.—Those who will enter our large cities to labor as medical evangelists must begin their work in a very wise way. Angels of God will make the impression, and under the hallowed influence of the Holy Spirit, hearts will be touched. The words of the speaker bringing the form of sound doctrine into actual contact with the hearer will result in the saving of souls.—Letter 4, 1910 (*A Call to Medical Evangelism and Health Education,* p. 42).

All Called to Have Part.—Medical missionary work is the helping hand of God. This work must be done. It is needed in new fields, and in fields where the work was started years ago. Since this work is the helping hand of God and the entering wedge of the gospel, we want you [church members] to understand that you are to have a part in it. It is not to be divorced from the gospel. Every soul before me this morning should be filled with the true medical missionary spirit.—*General Conference Bulletin,* April 7, 1903, p. 105 (*Review and Herald,* April 14, 1903).

Expansion of Health Evangelism Work Needed.—We thank the Lord for the medical missionary work that has already been done, but there is a large army of workers that is to engage in the same class of labor in different locations in cities, and the byways and hedges. There is more enlightenment to be given to those who are perishing in their sins. There will be very singular cases brought to notice who need not only the necessities of physical wants supplied, which is as essential as the first work, but to be brought into connection with sanitariums and homes that can present pure, correct principles for medical restoration. There are many who will catch hold of the hand stretched out to save them.—Letter 83, 1897.

COMBINE HUMANITARIAN SERVICE AND PERSONAL EVANGELISM

Health Ministry Work to Point Sick to Christ.—We should ever remember that the object of the medical missionary work is to point sin-sick men and women to the Man of Calvary, who taketh away the sin of the world. By beholding Him, they will be changed into His likeness. We are to encourage the sick and suffering to look to Jesus and live. Let the workers keep Christ, the Great Physician, constantly before those to whom disease of body and soul has brought discouragement. Point them to the One who can heal both physical and spiritual disease. . . .

God often reaches hearts through our efforts to relieve physical suffering.

Medical missionary work is the pioneer work of the gospel. . . .

In almost every community there are large numbers who do not listen to the preaching of God's word or attend any religious service. If they are [to be] reached by the gospel, it must be carried to their homes. Often the relief of their physical needs is the only avenue by which they can be approached. . . . Unselfish love, manifested in acts of disinterested kindness, will make it easier for these suffering ones to believe in the love of Christ. . . .

As they see one with no inducement of earthly praise or compensation come into their homes, ministering to the sick, feeding the hungry, clothing the naked, comforting the sad, and tenderly pointing all to Him of whose love and pity the human worker is but the messenger—as they see this, their hearts are touched. Gratitude springs up. Faith is kindled. They see that God cares for them, and they are prepared to listen as His word is opened.—*The Ministry of Healing,* pp. 144, 145. (1905)

DEMONSTRATING CHRIST'S CHARACTER

Health Evangelism Workers to Represent Christ's Character.—The medical missionary work is of divine origin, and has a most glorious mission to fulfill. In all its bearings it is to be in conformity with Christ's work. Those who are workers together with God will just as surely represent the character of Christ as Christ represented the character of His Father while in this world.—Manuscript 130, 1902 (*Medical Ministry,* p. 24).

Call to Be Christians Both in Profession and Practice.— Study the life and character of Christ, and seek to imitate His example. The unconsecrated course of some of those who claim to be believers in the third angel's message has resulted in driving some of the poor sheep into the desert; and who is it that has manifested a shepherd's care for the lost and wandering? Is it not time to be Christians in practice as well as profession? What benevolence, what compassion, what tender sympathy, Jesus has manifested toward suffering humanity! The heart that beats in unison with His great heart of infinite love will give sympathy to every needy soul, and will make it manifest that he has the mind of Christ. "A bruised reed shall He not break, and the smoking flax shall He not quench." Every suffering soul has a claim upon the sympathy of others, and those who are imbued with the love of Christ, filled with His pity, tenderness, and compassion, will respond to every appeal to their sympathy. They will not say, when an appeal is made to them in behalf of those who are perishing out of Christ, "This does not concern me." They will not act the part of the elder brother, but will manifest personal interest and sympathy. They will follow the example of their Master, and will go out to seek and to save that which was lost, obeying the Saviour's words when He said, "Love one another as I have loved you." Every soul who attempts to retrace his wanderings and return to God needs the help of those who have a tender, pitying heart of Christlike love.— *Review and Herald,* October 16, 1894.

Unselfish Deeds Are Strongest Argument for Christianity.— The truth expressed in living, unselfish deeds is the strongest argument for Christianity. Relieving the sick and helping the distressed is working in Christ's lines, and demonstrates most powerful gospel truths representing Christ's mission and work upon the earth. The knowledge of the art of relieving suffering humanity opens doors without number through which the truth can find lodgment in the heart, and souls are saved unto life, eternal life.—Letter 36, 1893 (*Manuscript Releases,* vol. 2, p. 240).

MEDICAL AND MINISTERIAL WORK
TO BE UNITED IN CITY EVANGELISM

Medical Work to Accompany Gospel Ministry.—In our large cities the medical missionary work must go hand in hand with the gospel ministry. It will open doors for the entrance of truth.—Manuscript 117, 1901 (*Evangelism,* p. 387).

Medical Work Not to Be Separated From Ministerial Work.—Of late [1899] a great interest has been aroused for the poor and outcast classes; a great work has been entered upon for the uplifting of the fallen and degraded. This in itself is a good work. We should ever have the spirit of Christ, and we are to do the same class of work that He did for suffering humanity. The Lord has a work to be done for the outcasts. There is no question but that it is the duty of some to labor among them, and try to save the souls that are perishing. This will have its place in connection with the proclamation of the third angel's message and the reception of Bible truth.—Manuscript 3, 1899 (*Evangelism,* p. 548).

Satan Tries to Divide Medical and Ministerial Work.— The medical missionary work is not to be carried forward as something apart from the work of the gospel ministry. The Lord's people are to be one. There is to be no separation in His work. Time and means are being absorbed in a work which is carried forward too earnestly in one direction. The Lord has not appointed this. He sent out His twelve apostles and afterward the Seventy to preach the word to the people, and He gave them power to heal the sick and to cast out devils in His name. The two lines of work must not be separated. Satan will invent every possible scheme to separate those whom God is seeking to make one. We must not be misled by his devices. The medical missionary work is to be connected with the third angel's message as the hand is connected with the body; and the education of students in medical missionary lines is not complete unless they are trained to work in connection with the church and the ministry.—Manuscript 3, 1899 (*Counsels on Health,* p. 557).

Ministers and Physicians to Work Together in City Evangelism.—In this effort in behalf of the cities, all classes of laborers may cooperate to advantage. Especially valuable is the help that the physician may render as an evangelist. If ministers and physicians will plan to unite in an effort to reach the honesthearted ones in the cities, the physicians, as well as the ministers, will be placed on vantage ground. As they labor in humility, God will open the way before them, and many will receive a saving knowledge of the truth.—*North Pacific Union Gleaner,* April 13, 1910.

PHYSICIANS AS GOSPEL MEDICAL MISSIONARIES

Physicians Symbolize Ministry of Gospel.—The work which He [Christ] gave to our physicians was to symbolize to the world the ministry of the gospel in medical missionary work.—*Testimonies for the Church,* vol. 6, p. 246. (1900)

Physicians to Present Message From Medical Perspective.—Those who are Christian physicians may do a precious work for God as medical missionaries. Too often so many things engage the minds of physicians that they are kept from the work that God would have them do as evangelists. Let the medical workers present the important truths of the third angel's message from the physician's viewpoint. Physicians of consecration and talent can secure a hearing in large cities at times when other men would fail. As physicians unite with ministers in proclaiming the gospel in the great cities of the land, their combined labors will result in influencing many minds in favor of the truth for this time.—*Review and Herald,* April 7, 1910 (*Medical Ministry,* p. 248).

BALANCE NEEDED

Medical Work Not to Be Exalted Above Ministerial Work.—You [Dr. J. H. Kellogg] cannot properly build up and manage the medical missionary work while giving it the prominence which you have thought that it should maintain. By representing the gospel ministry as inferior to the medical missionary work, you have placed a wrong mold upon that work. . . .

Not once or twice, but many times, the ministers have been presented to me as sitting before you in meetings; and you have made charges against them that have brought no credit to yourself. The impression left upon minds has been that you regarded your judgment as superior to that of others. But should your methods be followed by your brethren, in all things, they would not be walking in the way of the Lord.

Your speaking of the ministers before your classes, and exalting the medical missionary work above the work of the ministry, is bringing in a state of things that is not in harmony with the third angel's message. I was shown that angels veiled their faces when they heard your words in regard to God's servants. These men have been given a work to do for God, and many of them are doing this work just as faithfully as you are doing your work. Some are laboring under more discouraging circumstances, because they have not the advantages and facilities which you possess for the prosecution of their work.

The swaying of things so heavily in one line is not after the Lord's plan. . . .

The medical missionary work must be as closely connected with the work of the gospel ministry as the hand and arm are connected with the body. You need the gospel ministry to give prominence and stability to the medical missionary work; and the ministry needs the medical missionary work to demonstrate the practical working of the gospel. The Lord would have His work carried forward symmetrically and harmoniously. His message must be carried to all parts of the world. There is a large vineyard to be worked. The wise husbandman works the vineyard so that every part produces fruit.

Read the sixty-first chapter of Isaiah. This chapter will tell us what is the work before us. "The Lord hath anointed me to preach good tidings unto the meek; he hath sent me to bind up the brokenhearted, to proclaim liberty to the captives, and the opening of the prison to them that are bound; to proclaim the acceptable year of the Lord, and the day of vengeance of our God; to comfort all that mourn; to appoint unto them that mourn in Zion, to give unto them beauty for ashes, the oil of joy for mourning, the garment of praise for the spirit of heaviness; that they might be called trees of righteousness, the planting of the Lord, that he might be glorified."

Please consider what this . . . verse means, "And they shall build the old wastes, they shall raise up the former desolations, and they shall repair the waste cities, the desolations of many generations." . . .

The Lord moves in straight lines, and He will have each part of His work united with the other.—Letter 135, 1899 (portion in *Manuscript Releases,* vol. 4, pp. 131, 132).

Health Reform Unwisely Presented Creates Prejudices.— Health reform, wisely treated, will prove an entering wedge where the truth may follow with marked success. But to present health reform unwisely, making that subject the burden of the message, has served to create prejudice with unbelievers and to bar the way to the truth, leaving the impression that we are extremists. Now, the Lord would have us wise and understanding as to what is His will. We must not give occasion for us to be regarded [as] extremists. This will place us and the truth God has given us to bear to the people at a great disadvantage. Through weaving in unconsecrated self, that which we are ever to present as a blessing becomes a stumbling block.—Manuscript 5, 1881 (*Manuscript Releases,* vol. 2, p. 105).

MINISTRIES FOR THOSE WHO ARE ADDICTED

Those With Addictions Need to Be Helped.—Every true reform has its place in the work of the gospel and tends to the uplifting of the soul to a new and nobler life. . . .

There is everywhere a work to be done for those who through intemperance have fallen. . . . Through intemperate habits they bring upon themselves disease, and through greed to obtain money for sinful indulgence they fall into dishonest practices. Health and character are ruined. Aliens from God, outcasts from society, these poor souls feel that they are without hope either for this life or for the life to come. The hearts of the parents are broken. Men speak of these erring ones as hopeless; but not so does God regard them. He understands all the circumstances that have made them what they are, and He looks upon them with pity. This is a class that demand help. Never give them occasion to say, "No man cares for my soul." . . .

Often in helping the intemperate we must, as Christ so often did, give first attention to their physical condition. . . . In every city a place should be provided where the slaves of evil habit may receive help to break the chains that bind them. . . .

The self-indulgent must be led to see and feel that great moral renovation is necessary if they would be men. . . .

The tempted one needs to understand the true force of the will. This is the governing power in the nature of man—the power of decision, of choice. . . .

Through the right exercise of the will, an entire change may be made in the life. By yielding up the will to Christ, we ally ourselves with divine power. We receive strength from above to hold us steadfast. A pure and noble life, a life of victory over appetite and lust, is possible to everyone who will unite his weak, wavering human will to the omnipotent, unwavering will of God.—*The Ministry of Healing,* pp. 171-176. (1905)

Temperance Work* to Be Emphasized.—God wants us to stand where we can warn the people. He desires us to take up the temperance question. By wrong habits of eating and drinking, men are destroying what power they have for thought and intelligence.

---

* "Temperance work" now is often referred to as "substance abuse and recovery ministries."

We do not need to take an ax and break into their saloons. We have a stronger weapon than this—the word of the living God. That will cleave its way through the hellish shadow which Satan seeks to cast athwart their pathway. God is mighty and powerful. He will speak to their hearts. We have seen Him doing this.—*General Conference Bulletin,* April 23, 1901, pp. 424 (*Evangelism,* pp. 587, 588; *Temperance,* p. 235).

Temperance Work to Be Revived.—Consider how the evil of intemperance is at work in our cities. Do we not know that the liquor sold in the saloons of our land is drugged with the most poisonous substances?* We read of one and another who has taken life while under the influence of liquor—liquor that has robbed them of their reason. We need to have a knowledge of these things, that we may work intelligently to help others. The temperance cause needs to be revived as it has not yet been. We need to preach the gospel, that men and women may understand how to obey the word of God. It is the word of the living God that will bring men and women into right relation to Him; it will make impressions on heart and mind and character. Let every one of us be aroused to do the work that is waiting to be done—the work that Christ did when He was in the world. By beholding the works of Christ, humanity will take hold upon divinity. There the appeal to souls is made, and He never turns one away. Whatever may be the position in life, whatever the past may have been, He will still receive.—*Review and Herald,* January 14, 1909.

Temperance Includes All Aspects of Healthful Living.—In the advocacy of the cause of temperance, our efforts are to be multiplied. The subject of Christian temperance should find a place in our sermons in every city where we labor. Health reform in all its bearings is to be presented before the people, and special efforts made to instruct the youth, the middle-aged, and the aged in the

---

* A common practice at the time.

principles of Christian living.—Manuscript 61, 1909 (*Temperance*, p. 239).

Youth to Advance Temperance Ministry.—There is no class of persons capable of accomplishing more in the warfare against intemperance than are God-fearing youth. In this age the young men in our cities should unite as an army, firmly and decidedly to set themselves against every form of selfish, health-destroying indulgence. What a power they might be for good! How many they might save from becoming demoralized in the halls and gardens fitted up with music and other attractions to allure the youth! . . .

The young men and young women who claim to believe the truth for this time can please Jesus only by uniting in an effort to meet the evils that have, with seductive influence, crept in upon society. They should do all they can to stay the tide of intemperance now spreading with demoralizing power over the land. Realizing that intemperance has open, avowed supporters, those who honor God take their position firmly against this tide of evil by which both men and women are being swiftly carried to perdition.—*Youth's Instructor*, July 16, 1903 (*Temperance*, p. 235).

CARE FOR SINGLE MOTHERS, ORPHANS, AND THE ELDERLY

Widows, Orphans, Elderly, Helpless, and the Sick All Need Assistance.—When all has been done that can be done in helping the poor to help themselves, there still remain the widow and the fatherless, the aged, the helpless, and the sick, that claim sympathy and care. Never should these be neglected. They are committed by God Himself to the mercy, the love, and the tender care of all whom He has made His stewards.—*The Ministry of Healing*, p. 201. (1905)

Orphans and Elderly to Be Helped.—God calls upon us

to supply to these children, so far as we can, the want of a father's care. Instead of standing aloof, complaining of their faults, and of the trouble they may cause, help them in every way possible. Seek to aid the careworn mother. Lighten her burdens.

Then there are the multitudes of children who have been wholly deprived of the guidance of parents and the subduing influence of a Christian home. Let Christians open their hearts and homes to these helpless ones. The work that God has committed to them as an individual duty should not be turned over to some benevolent institution or left to the chances of the world's charity. If the children have no relatives able to give them care, let the members of the church provide homes for them. He who made us ordained that we should be associated in families, and the child nature will develop best in the loving atmosphere of a Christian home. . . .

The aged also need the helpful influences of the family. In the home of brethren and sisters in Christ can most nearly be made up to them the loss of their own home. . . . Make them feel that their help is valued, that there is something yet for them to do in ministering to others, and it will cheer their hearts and give interest to their lives.

So far as possible let those whose whitening heads and failing steps show that they are drawing near to the grave remain among friends and familiar associations. . . .

Whenever they are able to do so, it should be the privilege of the members of every family to minister to their own kindred. When this cannot be, the work belongs to the church, and it should be accepted both as a privilege and as a duty. All who possess Christ's spirit will have a tender regard for the feeble and the aged.—*The Ministry of Healing*, pp. 203, 204. (1905)

SALVATION ARMY
METHODS NOT TO BE IMITATED

Although Work of Salvation Army Not Ours, We Should Not Condemn Them.—The enemy is determined to mix error with truth. To do this he uses the opportunity given him by the debased class for whom so much labor and money are expended, the class whose appetites have been perverted through indulgence, whose souls have been abused, whose characters are misshapen and deformed, whose habits and desires are groveling, who think habitually upon evil. Such ones can be transformed in character; but how few there are with whom the work is thorough and lasting!

Some will be sanctified through the truth; but many make a superficial change in their habits and practices, and then suppose that they are Christians. They are received into church fellowship, but they are a great trouble and a great care. Through them Satan tries to sow in the church the seeds of jealousy, dishonesty, criticism, and accusing. Thus he tries to corrupt the other members of the church. The disposition that has mastered them from childhood, that led them to break away from all restraint and brought them down to degradation, still controls them. They are reported to be rescued, but too often time shows that the work done for them did not make them submissive children of God. At every supposed slight, resentful feelings rise. They cherish bitterness, wrath, malice. By their words and spirit they show that they have not been born again. Their tendencies are downward, tending to sensuality. They are untrustworthy, unthankful, unholy. Thus it is with all who have not been soundly converted. Every one of these marred characters, untransformed, becomes an efficient worker for Satan, creating dissension and strife.

The Lord has marked out our way of working. As a people we are not to imitate and fall in with Salvation Army methods. This is not the work that the Lord has given us to do. Neither is it our work to condemn them and speak harsh words against them. There are precious, self-sacrificing souls in the Salvation Army. We are to treat them kindly. There are in the Army honest souls, who are sincerely serving the Lord and who will see greater light, advancing to the acceptance of all truth. The Salvation Army workers are trying to save the neglected, downtrodden ones. Discourage them not.

Let them do that class of work by their own methods and in their own way. But the Lord has plainly pointed out the work that Seventh-day Adventists are to do. Camp meetings and tent meetings are to be held. The truth for this time is to be proclaimed. A decided testimony is to be borne. And the discourses are to be so simple that children can understand them.—*Testimonies for the Church,* vol. 8, pp. 184, 185. (1904)

Chapter 10

PLANTING CHURCHES IN THE CITIES

Churches to Be Planted in City After City.—When I look at the piles of buildings there are here [in Battle Creek], I feel sad at heart. If you [church leaders] had the missionary spirit, if you had gone out in accordance with the largeness of the message, in accordance with its breadth and importance, you would not have erected one half of the buildings you have here. You would have made plants in city after city, and God would have approved of your work. He does not like your administration. He does not like your nearness of sight. He wants you to open new fields, and for years He has been calling upon you to do this. This takes money and laborers; but I read in Daniel that they which turn many to righteousness shall shine forever and ever. We want to be in that company. We want to be among the shining ones in the kingdom of God. There we shall want to see those for whom we have prayed and worked. God help us.—*General Conference Bulletin,* April 5, 1901, p. 85.

Church Members to Benefit Others.—Upon all who believe, God has placed the burden of raising up churches. The express purpose of the church is to educate men and women to use their entrusted capabilities for the benefit of the world, to employ the means God has lent, for His glory. He has made human beings His stewards. They are to employ His entrusted talents in building up His work and enlarging His kingdom. Our churches, large and small, are not to be treated in such a way that they will be helplessly dependent upon ministerial aid. The members are to be so established in the faith that they will have an intelligent knowledge of true missionary work. They are to follow Christ's example, ministering to those around them. Faithfully they are to fulfill the vows made at their baptism, the vow that they will practice the lessons taught in the life of Christ. They are to work together to keep alive in the church the principles of self-denial and self-sacrifice, which Christ, His divinity clothed with humanity, followed in His work as a missionary. It is imparting the knowledge of Christ's love and tenderness that gives efficiency to all missionary operations.—*Pacific Union Recorder,* August 1, 1901.

PRIORITY GIVEN TO PLANTING NEW CONGREGATIONS

Churches to Be Organized; Larger Churches to Assist Smaller Ones.—I have often thought how much more abundantly we should be blessed if in the larger churches there were a well-organized band of workers, who would become missionaries to cities and towns, teaching others the precious lessons they have learned, of truth, of righteousness, of a judgment to come. All should be learners, but not ever learning and never coming to a knowledge of the truth. Be diligent students, and all the time practice what you learn. This will give you an experience which will be of the highest value to yourselves, and will surely benefit others. God has given us light, which He has commanded us to let shine; and if some souls embrace the truth in a locality, organize them into a church as soon as it can be wisely done, and let them do what they can to build a humble house of worship, as they have done in Willis [Michigan], which they can dedicate to God, and where they can invite His presence to be with them. He says, "Where two or three are gathered together in my name, there am I in the midst of them." Then let the larger churches which are free from debt come to the help of their sister churches, and give of their entrusted means toward these smaller places of worship, that the small churches may not be oppressed and discouraged under a load of debt. Let us not, like the priest and the Levite, pass by on the other side. What blessings would be meted out to the churches that help in this way, and what love on the part of the poorer churches, as they realized that they were watched over for good! And with this help freely and cheerfully rendered would come enlarged views of Christian helpfulness and duty. A bond of brotherhood, and love strong and tender, would be created between the members of the churches, large and small; and all petty jealousies and envies would be burned out by the love so substantially expressed.—*Review and Herald,* July 21, 1891.

Work to Continue Until Church Is Well Established.— Our workers are not branching out as they should in their efforts. Our leading men are not awake to the work that must yet be accomplished. When I think of the cities in which so little work has been done, in which there are so many thousands to be warned of the soon coming of the Saviour, I feel an intensity of desire to see men and women going forth to the work in the power of the Spirit, filled with Christ's love for perishing souls.

The heathen in the cities at our doors have been strangely neglected. Organized effort should be made to save them. We are now to work to convert the heathen who are in the midst of us—those who are living within the shadow of our doors. A new song is to be put in their mouths, and they are to go forth to impart to others now in darkness, the light of the third angel's message.

We all need to be wide awake, that, as the way opens, we may advance the work in the large cities. We are far behind in following the light given us to enter the cities and erect memorials for God. Step by step we are to lead souls into the full light of truth. Many are longing for spiritual food. We are to continue working until a church is organized and a humble house of worship built. I am greatly encouraged to believe that many persons not of our faith will help considerably by their means. The light given me is that in many places, especially in the great cities of America, help will be given by such persons.—*Pacific Union Recorder,* October 23, 1902.

Church and School to Be Built for New Congregations.— When a company of believers is raised up, careful provision should be made for the permanence and stability of the work. A house of worship will be needed, and a school where Bible instruction may be given to the people. The workers should not leave their field of labor without building a church and providing a schoolroom and a teacher. . . . All this has been presented before me as a panoramic view. I saw workmen building humble houses of worship. Those newly come to the faith were helping with willing hands, and those who had means were assisting with their means. A schoolroom was prepared for the children. Teachers were selected to go to this place. The number in the school was not large, but it was a happy beginning. I heard the songs of children and of parents. Except the Lord build the house, they labor in vain that build it. Except the Lord keep the city, the watchman waketh but in vain.— Manuscript 3, 1899 (*Australasian Union Conference Record,* July 26, 1899).

New Churches Increase Number of Available Workers.— We should seek in every place to raise up a company of believers who will unite with us in uplifting the standard of truth, and working for rich and poor. Then as churches are established, there will be an increase of helpers to labor for the destitute and the outcast.—Manuscript 3, 1899 (*Gospel Workers,* p. 436).

Money Better Spent Reaching Those Who Then Can Help Reach Others.—If the efforts, the talent, the labor, the money, which have been thrown into Chicago for the last several years had been appropriated toward acquainting with the truth of God for these last days a class of people who could have been reached with wise, well directed efforts, many would have received the truth who would now be working to give it to others of their own class.—Manuscript 46, 1900 (*Manuscript Releases,* vol. 4, p. 422).

Every City in America Should Have a Memorial for God.—Why are so many places passed by? Look upon the towns and cities yet unworked. There are many large cities in America, not only in the South, but in the North, yet to be worked. In every city in America there should be some memorial for God. But I could mention many places where the light of truth has not yet shone. The angels of heaven are waiting for human instrumentalities to enter the places where witness has not yet been borne to present truth. The Lord's name is reproached. Please read your Bibles, and see if it is not true that our work has scarcely begun.—*Review and Herald,* December 30, 1902.

Minister to Move to Different Field After a New Church Is Organized.—Young ministers should not be encouraged to preach to the churches. This is not their work. They are to go forth without the camp, taking up the work in places where the truth has not yet been proclaimed. Let them go in the humility and meekness of Christ, obtaining strength from the source of all strength. . . .

Ministers are not to spend their time laboring for those who have already accepted the truth. With Christ's love burning in their hearts, they are to go forth to win sinners to the Saviour. Beside all waters, God's messengers are to sow the seeds of truth. Place after place is to be visited; church after church is to be raised up. Those who take their stand for the truth are to be organized into churches, and then the minister is to pass on to other equally important fields.—*Review and Herald,* August 19, 1902.

Churches Weakened by Ministers Hovering Over Them.—The time that has been used in preaching to our churches has not strengthened them, but has made them weak and helpless, to be fed with milk and not with meat. God has been calling upon His ministers to leave the ninety and nine and hunt for the lost sheep. Your [Elder and Mrs. Stephen N. Haskell's] experience is to be a lesson for all who are hovering over the churches—consumers and not producers. We tell you to put your trust in God. Let Him guide you. The Lord Jesus is answering your prayers.—Letter 132, 1901 (*Manuscript Releases,* vol. 10, pp. 227, 228).

DO NOT COLONIZE

Many Small Centers Needed.—It is the Lord's desire that renewed efforts shall be put forth in many places, and small plants be established. A work is to be done that is to open the way for the advancement of the truth, and that will increase the faith of souls. . . .

There are many fields to be worked, and calculations should not be made to plant many large interests in a few favored localities. The Lord has instructed me that we are not to make many large centers; for in every field there should be facilities for the successful carrying on of the work. For this reason a few large institutions should not be allowed to exhaust all the income of means. In small and large cities, and in settlements that lie outside the cities, there should be maintained small centers where faithful watchmen are stationed who will labor for souls. Wherever the missionary worker goes, there should follow his efforts the establishment of some small plant that the advance of the work may be hastened. When God's servants do their work faithfully, Providence will open the way for these facilities in many places.—Letter 30, 1911 (*Evangelism,* p. 535).

Work to Be Done in Many Localities.—You [Dr. J. H. Kellogg] know that I have had light to the effect that there are altogether too many interests centered in Battle Creek. Progress ought to be made elsewhere. How many cities there are in America which have been left untouched! Why not let some of your energies be devoted to setting men at work in different localities? Let the influence of truth be far-reaching. Let the knowledge of how to preserve health be widely disseminated. Let work be begun where scarcely anything has been accomplished.—Letter 43, 1895 (*Manuscript Releases,* vol. 17, p. 309).

Not to Hide Away in Colonies.—This is no time to colonize. From city to city the work is to be carried quickly. The light that has been placed under a bushel is to be taken out and placed on a candlestick, that it may give forth light to all that are in the house.—Manuscript 21, 1910 (*Medical Ministry,* p. 302).

Members Who Congregate Together Called to Wider Service.—Time is fast passing. The day of the Lord's reckoning is approaching. Seventh-day Adventists are not to colonize. We are to work as Jesus has given us an example. Of the work of Christ we read: "And leaving Nazareth, he came and dwelt in Capernaum, which is upon the seacoast, in the borders of Zabulon and Nephthalim: that it might be fulfilled which was spoken by Esaias the prophet, saying, The land of Zabulon, and the land of Nephthalim, by the way of the sea, beyond Jordan, Galilee of the Gentiles; the people which sat in darkness saw great light; and to them which sat in the region and shadow of death light is sprung up." "And Jesus went about *all* Galilee, teaching in their synagogues, and preaching the gospel of the kingdom, and healing all manner of sickness and all manner of disease among the people." This is the work that will open doors for the truth. . . .

Thus was the time of the Great Missionary occupied. I think of the work that might be done if those held in Battle Creek and a few other favored places were carrying forward the work in the villages and towns and cities in which there are no memorials for the truth. . . .

When the eyes of the members of our large churches are anointed with the heavenly eyesalve, they will arise, and go forth to fulfill this commission. When their hearts are imbued with the Holy Spirit, they will worship the Lord their God, and Him only will they serve. The Lord is calling upon those who are congregated in congested centers to go forth into the places where the truth has never been proclaimed. They are to teach the things that Christ has commanded, leaving alone the various suppositions born of erratic theories. False teachers will come in, teaching for doctrine the commandments of men. Satan will bring forward fables to militate against the principles of Christ's teaching. God calls upon His faithful messengers to search His Word, and to teach only those things that Christ has commanded. . . .

There is too much hovering round our institutions, too much ease-loving. The commission of Christ is to be carried out to the letter. God's people must consecrate to Him their means and their capabilities. The faithful soldiers of the cross of Christ are to go forth without the camp, bearing the reproach, and following in the path of self-denial trodden by the Redeemer.

The ministers who are hovering over the churches, preaching to those who know the truth, would better go into places still in darkness. Unless they do this, they themselves and their congregations will become dwarfed. Our religion has become weak and sickly because the members of the church have left their first love. They might be strong men and women in Christ if they would obey the Lord's directions.

I am commanded to lift my voice in warning, and to call upon our people who are gathered together in Battle Creek to go forth and take up the work appointed them by God. The world is perishing in sin. How much longer will you allow yourselves to be held from the great, needy vineyard, when the history of this world is so near its close?—*Review and Herald,* February 9, 1905.

Centralizing Large Institutions Not Best.—Something has been done in foreign missions, and something in home missions; but altogether too much territory has been left unworked. The work is too much centralized. The interests in Battle Creek are overgrown, and this means that other portions of the field are robbed of facilities which they should have had. The larger and still larger preparations, in the erection and enlargement of buildings, which have called together and held so large a number in Battle Creek, are not in accordance with God's plan, but in direct contravention of His plan.

It has been urged that there were great advantages in having so many institutions in close connection, that they would be a strength to one another and could afford help to those seeking education and employment. This is according to human reasoning; it will be admitted that, from a human point of view, many advantages are gained by crowding so many responsibilities in Battle Creek; but the vision needs to be extended.

These interests should be broken up into many parts in order that the work may start in cities which it will be necessary to make centers of interest. Buildings should be erected and responsibilities centered in many localities that are now robbed of vital, spiritual interest in order to swell the overplus already in Battle Creek.— *Testimonies for the Church,* vol. 8, pp. 59, 60. (1904)

Members Clustered Together Lose Sense of Mission.— The word of the Lord has come to me that there are too many believers clustered in a few places and that many are losing their sense of the shortness of time and their burden to proclaim the third angel's message. There is to be true conversion of heart on the part of every such believer. Those who are connected with our offices of publication need especially to carry a burden for souls and to study ways and means of doing personal work in the highways and hedges.

The Lord is not glorified in the swelling of numbers that is seen in some of our centers of training and of missionary effort.— Manuscript 53, 1910.

Battle Creek Fires Allowed by God to Decentralize Church Institutions.—The Lord permitted fire to consume the principal buildings of the Review and Herald and the sanitarium,[*] and thus removed the greatest objection urged against moving out of Battle Creek. It was His design that instead of rebuilding the one large sanitarium, our people should make plants in several places.

---

[*] The Battle Creek Sanitarium burned on February 18, 1902; the Review and Herald Publishing Company burned on December 30, 1902.

These smaller sanitariums should have been established where land could be secured for agricultural purposes.—*Testimonies for the Church,* vol. 8, p. 227. (1904)

STRATEGY FOR CHURCH PLANTING

Pray for God's Guidance When Planting Churches.— We must seek wisdom of God, for by faith I see a strong church in that city [Palmerston, New Zealand]. Our work must be to watch and to pray, to seek counsel of the One wonderful and mighty in counsel. One mightier than the strongest powers of hell can take the prey from Satan, and under His guidance the angels of heaven will carry on the battle against all the powers of darkness and plant the standard of truth and righteousness in that city.—Letter 79, 1893 (*Evangelism,* p. 39).

Converts to Be Thoroughly Grounded in the Truth.— Wherever an effort is made to raise up a church, thorough and faithful instructions should be given to those who accept the truth. No part of the work should be neglected, and they should not be left to themselves when the laborer goes to a new field, but should still receive care and instruction. Let nothing be left in an incomplete, slipshod manner. Whatever is done should be done with thoroughness. The few who are thus brought into the truth will in time accomplish more than if there is a greater number uneducated, untrained, who do not realize their responsibility, and whose peculiarities are woven into their religious experience. It will be far more difficult to undo that which has been done wrong, and put another mold on the work, than to take the work from the very beginning.—*Review and Herald,* October 5, 1886.

IGNORE CRITICS

Unbalanced Members Undermine God's Work.—In all the history of the church, no reformation has been carried forward without encountering serious obstacles. Thus it was in Paul's day. Wherever the apostle would raise up a church, there were some who professed to receive the faith, but who brought in heresies that, if received, would eventually crowd out the love of the truth. Luther suffered great perplexity and distress from the course of fanatical persons who claimed that God had spoken directly through them, and who therefore set their own ideas and opinions above the testimony of the Scriptures. Many who were lacking in faith and experience, but who had considerable self-sufficiency, and who loved to hear and tell some new thing, were beguiled by the pretensions of the new teachers, and they joined the agents of Satan in their work of tearing down what God had moved Luther to build up. The Wesleys also, and others who blessed the world by their influence and their faith, encountered at every step the wiles of Satan in pushing overzealous, unbalanced, and unsanctified ones into fanaticism of every grade.—*The Spirit of Prophecy,* vol. 4, p. 245. (1884)

Chapter 11

THE WORK
IN SPECIFIC CITIES

Cities in North America

Work in America to Be Enlarged.—I wish to tell you, my dear friends, that the work here in America is to be greatly enlarged. So many times there is presented before me the work which ought to have been done in America, but which has not been done, that my soul is very heavily burdened. City after city should have been worked, and if this had been faithfully done, there would have been brought into the truth those who could have gone forth to win other souls to Christ. In every city there should be memorials for God. But the way in which the work has been managed has resulted in a depleted treasury. The lack of effort to plant the standard of truth in the cities of America has brought about a condition of things in which the consuming is larger than the producing; and how the work shall now be carried forward is a difficult problem.—Letter 20, 1903 (*Manuscript Releases*, vol. 7, p. 123).

NORTHEASTERN CITIES

Cities Impacted by 1844 Movement to Be Worked Again.—Instruction has been given me that the message should go again with power in the cities in the Eastern States. In many of the large cities of the East the first and second angels' messages were proclaimed during the 1844 movement. To us, as God's servants, has been entrusted the third angel's message, the binding-off message, that is to prepare a people for the coming of the King. We are to make every effort to give a knowledge of the truth to all who will hear, and there are many who will listen. All through the large cities God has honest souls who are interested in what is truth.—*Testimonies for the Church,* vol. 9, p. 98. (1909)

Third Angel's Message to Be Proclaimed in Cities of the Northeast.—All these cities of the East where the first and the second angels' messages were proclaimed with power, and where the third angel's message was preached in the early days of our history as a separate, peculiar people, must now be worked anew. There is Portland, Maine; there is Boston, and all the many towns round about; there is New York City, and the populous cities close by; there is Philadelphia and Baltimore and Washington. I need not enumerate all these places; you know where they are. The Lord desires us to proclaim the third angel's message with power in these cities.

We cannot exercise this power ourselves. All we can do is to choose men of capability, and urge them to go into these avenues of opportunity, and there proclaim the message in the power of the Holy Spirit.—Manuscript 53, 1909.

Church Members in the West to Support Evangelism in the East.—As we labor faithfully in our neighborhoods and in the towns close by, and as we bear a decided message in the great cities of our land, we shall see of the salvation of God. . . .

The truth is to go forth as a lamp that burneth in the cities of the East, and our brethren in the West now have the privilege of advancing the cause of God in that portion of the field where the third angel's message was first proclaimed.—Manuscript 23, 1910.

Boston, Massachusetts

Work Should Include Boston.—I am instructed that Boston must be worked; and I know that the possession of this sanitarium site is one of the greatest blessings that could come to our work in the Eastern States.—*Review and Herald,* September 29, 1904.

Thousands in Boston Waiting to Hear the Truth.—I feel

a deep anxiety that Boston shall hear the word of the Lord and the reasons of our faith. Ask the Lord to raise up laborers to enter the field. . . . There are thousands in Boston craving for the simple truth as it is in Jesus.—*Special Testimonies,* Series B, No. 13, p. 8. (1908)

Message to Go With Power.—If in the city of Boston and other cities of the East, you [Dr. Daniel H. Kress] and your wife will unite in medical evangelistic work, your usefulness will increase, and there will open before you clear views of duty. In these cities the message of the first angel went with great power in 1842 and 1843, and now the time has come when the message of the third angel is to be proclaimed extensively in the East. There is a grand work before our Eastern sanitariums. The message is to go with power as the work closes up.—Letter 20, 1910 (*Counsels on Health,* p. 547).

Medical Work to Be Done in Boston and Other New England Cities.—When the New England Sanitarium was removed from South Lancaster [Massachusetts] to Melrose [Massachusetts], the Lord instructed me that this was in the order of His opening providence. The buildings and grounds at Melrose are of a character to recommend our medical missionary work, which is to be carried forward not only in Boston, but in many other unworked cities in New England. The Melrose property is such that conveniences can be provided that will draw to that sanitarium persons not of our faith. The aristocratic as well as the common people will visit that institution to avail themselves of the advantages offered for restoration of health.

Boston has been pointed out to me repeatedly as a place that must be faithfully worked. The light must shine in the outskirts and in the inmost parts. The Melrose Sanitarium is one of the greatest agencies that can be employed to reach Boston with the truth. The city and its suburbs must hear the last message of mercy to be given to our world. Tent meetings must be held in many places. The workers must put to the very best use the abilities God has given them. The gifts of grace will increase by wide use. But there must be no self-exaltation. No precise lines are to be laid down. Let the Holy Spirit direct the workers. They are to keep looking unto Jesus, the Author and Finisher of their faith. The work for this great city will be signalized by the revelation of the Holy Spirit, if all will walk humbly with God. . . .

We hope that those in charge of the work in New England will cooperate with the Melrose Sanitarium managers in taking aggressive steps to do the work that should be done in Boston. A hundred workers could be laboring to advantage in different portions of the city, in varied lines of service.—*Special Testimonies,* Series B, No. 13, pp. 12, 13 (*Counsels on Health,* pp. 554, 555). (1908)

New York City

New York Businessmen to Be Given the Message.—You should feel a decided responsibility for the working of New York City. The men in the business houses of New York and other large cities, as verily as the heathen in foreign lands, must be reached with the message. The enemy would be rejoiced to see the grand, saving truth for this time confined to a few places. He is not inactive. He is instilling into the minds of men his deceptive theories to blind their eyes and confuse their understanding, that the saving truth may not be brought to their knowledge. Soon the Sunday laws will be enforced, and men in positions of trust will be embittered against the little handful of God's commandment-keeping people.—Letter 168, 1909 (*Manuscript Releases,* vol. 4, pp. 278, 279).

Sanitarium and School Needed Near New York City and Other Cities.—We need a sanitarium and a school in the vicinity of New York City, and the longer the delay in the securing of these, the more difficult it will become.

It would be well to secure a place as a home for our mission workers outside of the city. It is of great importance that they have the advantages of pure water, free from all contamination. For this reason, it is often well to consider the advantages of locations among the hills. . . .   A place in the city should also be secured where simple treatments might be administered. . . .

Let such homes be secured in the neighborhood of several cities, and earnest, determined efforts be put forth by capable men to give in these cities the warning message that is to go to all the world. We have only touched, as it were, a few of the cities.—Letter 168, 1909 (*Medical Ministry*, p. 308).

Important to Establish Medical Missionary Work.—To start medical missionary work in New York will be the best thing that you [Elder and Mrs. Stephen N. Haskell] can do. I have been shown that if in this work there could be men and women of experience, who would give a correct representation of true medical missionary work, it would have great power in making a correct impression on the people.—Letter 195, 1901 (*Evangelism*, p. 387).

Workers Needed, Restaurants to Be Established.— While in New York in the winter of 1901, I received light in regard to the work in that great city. Night after night the course that our brethren should pursue passed before me. In Greater New York the message is to go forth as a lamp that burneth. God will raise up laborers for this work, and His angels will go before them. Though our large cities are fast reaching a condition similar to the condition of the world before the Flood, though they are as Sodom for wickedness, yet there are in them many honest souls, who, as they listen to the startling truths of the advent message, will feel the conviction of the Spirit. New York is ready to be worked. In that great city the message of truth will be given with the power of God. The Lord calls for workmen. He calls upon those who have gained an experience in the cause to take up and carry forward in His fear the work to be done in New York and in other large cities of America. He calls also for means to be used in this work.

It was presented to me that we should not rest satisfied because we have a vegetarian restaurant in Brooklyn, but that others should be established in other sections of the city. The people living in one part of Greater New York do not know what is going on in other parts of that great city. Men and women who eat at the restaurants established in different places will become conscious of an improvement in health. Their confidence once gained, they will be more ready to accept God's special message of truth.—*Testimonies for the Church,* vol. 7, pp. 54, 55.   (1902)

Honest-hearted People in City Need to Be Reached.— And there is New York, that great and wicked city. Who has carried the burden for that field? Who has felt the necessity of denying self that the work in that city may be carried forward? It is indeed a wicked city, but God had a Lot in Sodom, and He has a people in New York, who, as the hart panteth after the water brooks, are panting after the pure waters of Lebanon. New York is ready to be worked. When I was last there, just before leaving this country for Australia, the Lord showed me that His work should be established in New York. He showed me what could be done there if everyone would come up to His help. The power of God is to carry the truth in this city.

There is not a dearth of means among our people any more than there has been in the past. There is certainly not a dearth of means among our people in California. But in spite of this, the great field of New York is left untouched, while week after week, a large congregation meets here in the [Battle Creek] Tabernacle. The people ought to feel that the rebuke of God rests upon them because they are not working for Him in places which know not the truth. If they had the spirit of the pilgrim fathers, they would go forth to work for God in the waste places of the earth.—*General Conference Bulletin,* April 10, 1901, pp. 183, 184.

Borrow Funds at Interest Rather Than Stop the Work.— Rather than have the work in New York interrupted, I would hire [i.e., borrow] money and pay interest on it, in order to carry the work forward.—Letter 141, 1901 (*Manuscript Releases,* vol. 4, p. 319).

Thousands Waiting to Hear the Message.—In New York there are many who are ripe for the harvest. In this great city there are thousands who have not bowed the knee to Baal. The angel said, "Behold, I bring you good tidings of great joy, which shall be to all people." New York contains a part of the "all people." We desire to see the new year open with teachers at work in all parts of New York. There is a work to be done in this city—a work that ought to have been done twelve years ago. It was not done; and why? Because men and women were not awake to the importance of the time in which we are living. They were unprepared to do the work that needed to be done. Those who were unconverted in regard to health reform could not work in God's order. Therefore it is that in 1901 there is a dearth of workers.—Manuscript 117, 1901 (portion in *Evangelism,* p. 387).

Multiethnic Work to Be Conducted.—In New York City, in Chicago, and in other great centers of population, there is a large foreign element—multitudes of various nationalities, and all practically unwarned. Among Seventh-day Adventists there is a great zeal—and I am not saying there is any too much—to work in foreign countries; but it would be pleasing to God if a proportionate zeal were manifested to work the cities close by. His people need to move sensibly. They need to set about this work in the cities with serious earnestness. Men of consecration and talent are to be sent into these cities and set to work. Many classes of laborers are to unite in conducting these efforts to warn the people.—*Review and Herald,* October 29, 1914 (*Christian Service,* p. 199).

Work New York City Now, Utilizing Various Methods.—The best time to work New York City is now, the present *now;* and let the path be made as straight as possible for the work to be done, and at the same time let all be interested in every interest created in adjoining localities. . . .

The work in Greater New York is to be carried on in a way that will properly represent the sacredness and holiness of the truth of God. Vegetarian restaurants, treatment rooms, and cooking schools are to be established. The people are to be taught how to prepare wholesome food. They are to be shown the need of discarding tea, coffee, and flesh-meat.

Greater New York must stand in a different relation to the General Conference than the surrounding territory and interests which are different, and will have to be considered in a different light as far as missionary work is concerned. Greater New York is a world of itself, and should have in some respects different management from that of the surrounding localities.

God has His appointed agencies for the enlargement of our circle of influence, and for the increasing of the number of workers who will be missionaries indeed—laborers for the saving of the souls of their fellow-men. Those should set no boundaries to limit the sphere of their labors. The Christian church will ever meditate advance moves; it will ever be educating workers for further conquests for Christ. It should ever be moving on and on, that the truth may extend to all parts of the globe. . . .

The Lord would have had New York with all its surrounding localities and cities worked many years ago, and now that the opportunity is more plainly revealed, in all localities, in every church, hearts should be drawn out and connected with the progress of the gospel message. In all the neglected parts of the vineyard hearts should be thrilled with a genuine, living experience; and now that there is a great work started, no one must fold his hands, but all must regard with interest every movement of the church.

The churches now in different parts of Greater New York are to feel their sacred, God-given responsibilities. The word of the Lord is for this wide missionary field to be faithfully worked, and every vestige of criticism and fault-finding and separating of brethren to cease. The prejudices, their thinking and speaking evil, are to be put away. God will not tolerate any longer the spirit that has been controlling matters in our New York churches. The fields here are ready for harvest. In whatever direction we look our brethren must do their appointed work, which stretches to a large, unmeasured circumference. Those who would cherish and foster prejudice are not to be listened to. The work is to go forward under the direction of God, and those who wish to keep up the spirit of dissension should take themselves out of the way, and let God's work move onward.—*Important Testimony* (Pamphlet 038), pp. 6-9. (1903)

Nearby Cities, Trenton and Brooklyn, to Be Worked.— I am deeply impressed that Trenton [New Jersey] will be a central interest, as well as Brooklyn [New York], and still other localities outside the city of New York. We see indeed the fields in every direction in and outside of New York to be worked. There should be a hall secured to call the people together in New York City, and from surrounding localities out of New York City. . . .

God now wants our cities to be worked through the endowed, sanctified influences brought to bear upon the human mind. Transformation of one human mind means, if God's will is carried out, the transformation of many human minds. "None of us liveth to himself." None of us planneth to obtain glory to himself. The Lord gave Christ to our world, and with Christ He withheld nothing that could aid man in his humanity. When the organized church has withheld nothing of [its] entrusted talents and influence—when the Lord gave Christ, and then called for man to put that power and influence under the power of the gift of the Holy Spirit to crown his work with success, to make their [combined] work a signal success—should man fail on his part? . . .

What does the church propose to do in Christian instrumentality for the conversion of the world? The Lord calls for His memorials to be established in every city. There must be in every city the work which must be taken up to diffuse the influence of the truth, which has a sanctifying power upon those who hear and will respond.—Letter 183, 1901.

MID-ATLANTIC CITIES

Philadelphia, Pennsylvania
Evangelists to Work Where Religious Issues Agitate Citizens.—Philadelphia and other important places should be worked. Evangelists should be finding their way into all the places where the minds of men are agitated over the question of Sunday legislation and of the teaching of religion in the public schools. It is the neglect of Seventh-day Adventists to improve these providential opportunities to present the truth that burdens my heart and keeps me awake night after night.—*Review and Herald,* April 20, 1905 (*Evangelism,* pp. 394, 395).

Working Under Holy Spirit's Guidance Brings Results.—We should be pleased to see special work done in Philadelphia and in Boston. Many souls will be converted if men and women will do the personal work that needs to be done. By means of workers who labor under the influence of the Holy Spirit, many souls will be brought to a knowledge of the truth.—Manuscript 162, 1905 (*Manuscript Releases,* vol. 10, p. 228).

Washington, D.C.
Few in Capital of United States Have Been Warned.—I have been writing much in regard to the need of making more decided efforts in Washington, D.C. Light has been given me that something should be done in this city at once. How strange it is that at the very heart of the nation so little has been done to represent the loyalty of the people of God. To us has been given the grandest truth ever committed to mortals. Washington, the capital of the United States, is the very place from which this truth should shine forth. But what has been done there to proclaim the truth? What excuse can we give to God for our unfaithful stewardship?—Letter 132, 1903.

Workers Not to Be Relocated During Evangelistic Meetings.—A strong evangelistic effort must be put forth in the capital of the nation. . . .

I rejoice that you [Elder W. W. Prescott] have taken up this evangelistic work in Washington, and that so deep an interest has already been aroused. The accounts given regarding the work there correspond as nearly as possible to the representation given me of what would be. I am sure, for the matter has been presented to me, and this work must not be weakened by the necessary laborers' being called to other places. . . .

Evangelistic work must be done in Washington, and it must not be broken into by calls from other places. God would have His work in the highways carried forward in straight lines.

You are where the Lord would have you. Elder [A. G.] Daniells and yourself must not be loaded down with a great many burdens. Washington has been neglected long enough. A decided work must now be done there. The Lord will give strength and grace. The workers must not allow themselves to be diverted from the work by the many things that will be sure to press for attention. This is the reason that I have felt anxious that every talent of the workers in Washington shall be used in a way that will best advance His work.—Letter 53, 1904 (*Evangelism,* p. 395).

Personal Work Needed in the Cities.—I call upon the believers in Washington to come up to the help of the Lord, to the help of the Lord against the mighty powers of darkness. Personal labor will be needed in this city and its suburbs. Clear the King's highway. Lift up the standard higher and still higher. There is evangelistic work to be done in Washington and Baltimore and in the many other large cities of the South and the East. Let the work of teaching and healing be combined. Let ministers and medical missionaries put on the whole armor of God and go forth to proclaim the gospel message. A decided message is to be proclaimed in Washington. The trumpet is to be given a certain sound.—Letter 304, 1908 (*Evangelism,* p. 397).

*Takoma Park, Washington, D.C.**

Donations to Help Support Workers Near Washington, D.C.—We plead that those settled in Takoma Park shall become laborers together with God in planting the standard of truth in unworked territories. Let a part of the large donations called for be used to furnish workers in our cities close by Washington. Let faithful house-to-house work be done. Souls are perishing out of the ark of safety. Let the standard of truth be lifted up by the church members in their neighborhoods. Let ministers pitch their tent, and preach the truth to the people with power, and then move to another vicinity and preach the truth there.—Letter 94a, 1909 (*Evangelism*, p. 397).

Area Around Washington, D.C., to Be Worked.—Last Sunday we took a long drive through the district immediately adjoining our land [Takoma Park]. Sister Daniells was with us, and she showed us the settlements of people nearest our land. We were very much pleased with the appearance of these settlements. The houses are neat and comfortable and are surrounded with pretty yards.

The places that we saw reminded me of what we saw when we first visited Oakland and San Francisco. Then Oakland was not nearly as large as it is now. It was called San Francisco's bedroom, because so many of the businessmen working in San Francisco had homes in Oakland. Takoma Park might properly be called one of Washington's bedrooms. A great many businessmen live here, going to their work in the city each morning and returning at night to the quiet and retreat of the country. . . .

I am so thankful that our work is to be established in this place. Were Christ here upon the ground, He would say to us, "Lift up your eyes, and look on the fields; for they are white already to har-

---

* The General Conference was located in Takoma Park, a suburb of Washington, D.C., from 1904 to 1989; the Review and Herald Publishing Association was located there from 1906 to 1982.

vest." We have a work to do in leading precious souls onward step by step. . . .

My hopes for this place are high, as they have been in the past when I have entered new fields. The country for miles and miles around Washington is to be worked. We will not talk of what might have been done had the money spent in a few places been used in establishing memorials for God where such memorials are greatly needed; we will turn to the present. We want to present the truth in love and faith and hope and courage. . . .

We fully believe that the Lord has gone before us in the purchase of this land, and we shall do all in our power to carry out His will in the establishment of His work in this place. We shall need young people of the very best talent in our work in Washington. . . . The message must be proclaimed in Washington, and must go forth from that place to the other cities of the South. . . .

Last Sabbath I spoke in the Takoma Hall, which was well filled. I spoke from the fifteenth chapter of John, and my own soul was refreshed as I dwelt upon this important subject. A number of the citizens were present, and the owner of the hall was there also.

On Sunday I spoke in the M Street Memorial Church to the company of workers who have gathered in Washington to hold tent meetings and to do Bible work. My heart is filled with a longing desire that all who connect with this important work shall themselves have a daily experience in the things of God, that they may fill the place assigned them in the way that will win the Lord's approval. They are to be thorough in all that they do. On this point we cannot be too urgent. . . .

A great interest should be shown by our people in America in the extension of the Lord's work. They should feel a deep sense of grief and humiliation as they think that the cities that have been kept before them for the last twenty-five years have not yet heard the message of present truth. There are heathen, as it were, right in our borders, in our large cities. But who has a burden for these unwarned ones? Who is willing to invest [his] means in the work of enlightening them?—Manuscript 38, 1904.

MIDWESTERN CITIES

Chicago, Illinois

Chicago to Be Worked From Rural Location.—For the present, some will be obliged to labor in Chicago; but these should be preparing working centers in rural districts, from which to work the city. The Lord would have His people looking about them, and securing humble, inexpensive places as centers for their work. And from time to time larger places will come to their notice, which they will be able to secure at a surprisingly low price.—Manuscript 33, 1906 (*Medical Ministry,* pp. 305, 306).

Ethnic Work to Be Conducted in All Large Cities.—We drove out to see the newly established Swedish Mission on Oak Street [in Chicago]. There we were shown a building which our Swedish brethren, under the leadership of Elder S. Mortenson, have recently purchased for the headquarters of their work in Chicago. The building presents a good appearance. In the basement they have a well-equipped vegetarian restaurant. On the first floor there is a pleasant, commodious hall for meetings, comfortably seated for a congregation of about one hundred and fifty, and the two upper stories are rented to lodgers. I was indeed glad to see this evidence of progress in the Swedish work in Chicago.

There is a great work to be done for the people of all nations in the large cities in America, and such rallying points as this may be a great help in the matter of gaining the attention of the people, and in the training of workers. In every large city in America there are people of different nationalities, who must hear the message for this time. I long to see evidence that the lines of work which the Lord has marked out are being disinterestedly taken up. A work similar to that which is being done in Chicago for the Swedish people should be done in many places.—*Review and Herald,* February 9, 1905 (*Evangelism,* p. 572).

Caution Regarding Buying Property in Cities.—Scenes

that would soon take place in Chicago and other large cities also passed before me. As wickedness increased and the protecting power of God was withdrawn there were destructive winds and tempests. Buildings were destroyed by fire and shaken down by earthquakes. . . .

Some time after this I was shown that the vision of buildings in Chicago and the draft upon the means of our people to erect them, and their destruction, was an object lesson for our people, warning them not to invest largely of their means in property in Chicago, or any other city, unless the providence of God should positively open the way and plainly point out duty to build or buy as necessary in giving the note of warning. A similar caution was given in regard to building in Los Angeles. Repeatedly I have been instructed that we must not invest means in the erection of expensive buildings in cities.—Manuscript 33, 1906 (*Last Day Events*, pp. 113, 114).

Gospel to Be Clearly Presented in Localities Outside Chicago.—I have been given a representation of the preaching of the word of truth with clearness and power in many places where it has never yet been heard. The Lord would have the people warned; for a great work will be done in a short time. I have heard the word of God proclaimed in many localities outside the city of Chicago. There were many voices proclaiming the truth with great power. That which they proclaimed was not fanciful theories, but the warning message. While the solid truth of the Bible came from the lips of men who had no fanciful theories or misleading science to present, there were others who labored with all their power to bring in false theories regarding God and Christ. And miracles were wrought, to deceive, if possible, the very elect.—Manuscript 33, 1906 (*Medical Ministry*, p. 305).

Denver, Colorado

Despite Challenges, Work to Be Done in Denver.—As the matter is laid open before me, I see that there is need of substantial work being done in Denver. In the past many things have worked against the prosperity of the work there, and this unfavorable influence is not yet entirely removed.—Letter 84, 1901 (*Evangelism,* p. 402).

SOUTHERN CITIES

Nashville, Tennessee

Message to Be Conducted in Simplicity.—For the work in and about Nashville, we should do all we can to put it on a solid basis. The work should be conducted with simplicity, and in a way that will recommend the truth. There are many places in the South open to our work; but by all means let us make a beginning in the important cities, and carry the message now. "For thus saith the Lord of hosts; Yet once, it is a little while, and I will shake the heavens, and the earth, and the sea, and the dry land; and I will shake all nations, and the Desire of all nations shall come: and I will fill this house with glory, saith the Lord of hosts."—*Special Testimonies,* Series B, No. 11, p. 4. (1908)

New Orleans, Louisiana

Workers to Have Best Interest of Work at Heart.—New Orleans is to be worked. At a proper time of the year a public effort is to be made there. Camp meetings are to be held in many places, and evangelistic work is to be done after the camp meeting is over. Thus the sheaves are to be gathered in.

Now that the work in New Orleans is to be more fully entered upon, I am bidden to say, Let men and women who have a knowledge of the truth, and understand the way of the Lord, enter this city to work with wisdom and in the fear of the Lord. The laborers who are chosen for the work in New Orleans should be those who have the good of the cause at heart, men who will keep the glory of God always in view, and who will make the strength of the God of Israel their front guard and their rearward. The Lord will certainly hear and answer the prayers of His workers if they will seek

Him for counsel and instruction.—Manuscript 49, 1907 (*Evangelism*, p. 399).

Go Work the Cities Instead of Criticizing Those Already Working There.—The Lord God has been at work. My brethren, instead of criticizing what has been done, save your speech for the great cities that have not yet been worked, such as New Orleans, Memphis, and St. Louis. Go to these places and labor for the people, but do not speak a word of censure regarding those who have tried so hard to do everything in their power for the advancement of the work. Sometimes these workers would be almost discouraged, but we kept praying for them. Wherever I was, I would ask the prayers of God's people in their behalf.—*Review and Herald,* May 25, 1905 (*Evangelism,* p. 401).

WESTERN CITIES

California Cities
Focus Energies on Upbuilding Cause of God.—In my last vision I was shown that we should have a part to act in California in extending and confirming the work already commenced. I was shown that missionary labor must be put forth in California, Australia, Oregon, and other territories far more extensively than our people have imagined, or ever contemplated and planned. I was shown that we do not at the present time move as fast as the opening providence of God leads the way. I was shown that the present truth might be a power in California if the believers in the message would give no place to the enemy in unbelief and selfishness, but would concentrate their efforts to one object— the upbuilding of the cause of present truth.—*Life Sketches of Ellen G. White,* pp. 209, 210. (1874, 1915)

Ministers Need to Realize God's Call to Evangelize Cities in California.—Shall we not do all in our power to establish the work in the great cities of San Francisco and Oakland, and in all the other cities of California? Thousands upon thousands who live in the cities close by us need help in various ways. Let the ministers of the gospel realize that the Lord Jesus Christ said to His disciples, "Ye are the light of the world."—Manuscript 79, 1900 (*Evangelism,* p. 403).

Redlands and Other Southern California Cities to Be Worked.—Years ago many places in southern California were presented to me as very important fields, needing earnest labor. While at Redlands, I recognized it as one of these places. Light was given me that the unworked condition of the cities of southern California is a dishonor to those who know the truth. Recently Elder [William Ward] Simpson held tent meetings in Redlands, as a result of which many new members were added to the church. For this we praise the Lord. But there is still much to be done in Redlands. We need now to put forth earnest efforts in the cities of southern California.—*Review and Herald,* April 6, 1905.

Restaurants and Treatment Rooms to Be Established in Tourist Resort Cities.—When in Los Angeles I was instructed that not only in various sections of that city, but in San Diego and in other tourist resorts of Southern California, health restaurants and treatment rooms should be established. Our efforts in these lines should include the great seaside resorts. As the voice of John the Baptist was heard in the wilderness, "Prepare ye the way of the Lord," so must the voice of the Lord's messengers be heard in the great tourist and seaside resorts.—*Testimonies for the Church,* vol. 7, pp. 55, 56. (1902)

All Sections of San Francisco and Oakland Need to Be Evangelized.—There is a work to be done in California, a work that has been strangely neglected. Let this work be delayed no longer. As doors open for the presentation of truth, let us be ready to enter. Some work has been done in the large city of San Francisco, but as we study the field we see plainly that only a beginning has been made. As soon as possible, well-organized efforts should be put forth in different sections of this city and also in Oakland. The wickedness of San Francisco is not realized. Our work in this city must broaden and deepen. God sees in it many souls to be saved.—*Testimonies for the Church,* vol. 7, p. 110. (1902)

God's Work in San Francisco to Broaden and Deepen.—It would be difficult to describe my feelings as I stood before the San Francisco Church, Sabbath, November 10 [1900], and looked over the large congregation. My mind went back to the time, twenty-four years ago, when my husband and I were planning for the building of a house of worship in San Francisco. Some, when they saw the plan, said, "It is too large. The house will never be filled." At the same time we were erecting the first building of the Pacific Press and the meeting house in Oakland. How great was the anxiety felt, and how earnest the prayers offered to God that He would open the way for the advancement of these enterprises!

At that time I dreamed that I saw two bee hives, one in San Francisco and one in Oakland. In the hive in Oakland the bees were diligently at work. Then I looked at the hive in San Francisco, and saw very little being done. The hive in Oakland seemed to be far the more promising. After a time my attention was again called to the hive in San Francisco, and I saw that an entire change had taken place. Great activity was seen among the bees. They were earnestly at work.

When I related this dream, it was interpreted to mean that in San Francisco there was a great work to be done. . . .

We prayed much in regard to the necessities of the cause and the meaning of the dream, and resolved to venture out in accordance with the light given. My husband and I decided to sell our property in Battle Creek, that we might use the proceeds in this work. . . . This was done, and we helped to build the churches in Oakland and San Francisco. And the Lord revealed to us that although at first the work in San Francisco would move slowly, yet it would make steady advancement, and San Francisco would become a great center. The Lord would inspire men by His Holy Spirit to carry forward the work with faith and courage and perseverance. . . .

When we entered the San Francisco Church Sabbath morning we found it crowded to its utmost capacity. As I stood before the people, I thought of the dream and the instruction which had been given me so many years ago, and I was much encouraged. Looking at the people assembled, I felt that I could indeed say, The Lord has fulfilled His word. After I had finished speaking, all who wished to give themselves to the Lord in solemn consecration were invited to come forward. To this invitation two hundred persons responded. . . .

We earnestly hope that the steps taken in the future in the work in San Francisco will still be steps of progress. The work that has been done there is but a beginning. San Francisco is a world in itself, and the Lord's work there is to broaden and deepen. . . .

There is a great work to be done in San Francisco and Oakland. The Lord will use humble men in these great cities. . . .

There are men and women whom the Lord, through peculiar circumstances, will bring to the front in His work.—*Australasian Union Conference Record,* March 1, 1901.

CANADA

Toronto

Toronto to Be Worked.—My heart aches as I see the work needed to be done and no one to do it. We ought to fast and pray that the Lord will raise up laborers to go into the harvest field. What shall we do for workers? Elder [Daniel T.] Bourdeau says Toronto is an excellent field [in which] to labor. There are some choice souls cut upon the truth. Someone should be sent into this field.—Letter 26, 1883.

Cities Outside North America

Message to Be Translated So All Nations Can Receive the Truth.—A great work is committed to those who present the truth in Europe....There are France and Germany, with their great cities and teeming population. There are Italy, Spain, and Portugal, after so many centuries of darkness, . . . opened to the word of God—opened to receive the last message of warning to the world. There are Holland, Austria, Romania, Turkey, Greece, and Russia, the home of millions upon millions, whose souls are as precious in the sight of God as our own, who know nothing of the special truths for this time. . . .

A good work has already been done in these countries. There are those who have received the truth, scattered as light bearers in almost every land. . . .

But how little has been done in comparison with the great work before us! Angels of God are moving upon the minds of the people, and preparing them to receive the warning. Missionaries are needed in fields that have yet been scarcely entered. New fields are constantly opening. The truth must be translated into different languages, that all nations may enjoy its pure, life-giving influences. . . .

Colporteurs are meeting with encouraging success in the sale of our books. The light is thus brought to the people, while the colporteur—who in many cases has been thrown out of employment by accepting the truth—is enabled to support himself, and the sales are a financial help to the office. In the days of the Reformation, monks who had left their convents, and who had no other means of support, traversed the country, selling Luther's works, which were thus rapidly circulated throughout Europe. Colportage work was one of the most efficient means of spreading the light then, and so it will prove now.—*Review and Herald,* December 6, 1887 (*Life Sketches of Ellen G. White,* pp. 304, 305).

Some Countries Easier to Work Than Others.—Certain countries have advantages that mark them as centers of education and influence. In the English-speaking nations and the Protestant nations of Europe it is comparatively easy to find access to the people, and there are many advantages for establishing institutions and carrying forward our work. In some other lands, such as India and China, the workers must go through a long course of education before the people can understand them, or they the people. And at every step there are great difficulties to be encountered in the work. In America, Australia, England, and some other European countries, many of these impediments do not exist. America has many institutions to give character to the work. Similar facilities should be furnished for England, Australia, Germany, and Scandinavia, and other Continental countries as the work advances. In these countries the Lord has able workmen, laborers of experience. These can lead out in the establishment of institutions, the training of workers, and the carrying forward of the work in its different lines. God designs that they shall be furnished with means and facilities. The institutions established would give character to the work in these countries, and would give opportunity for the training of workers for the darker heathen nations. In this way the efficiency of our experienced workers would be multiplied a hundredfold.—*Testimonies for the Church,* vol. 6, p. 25. (1900)

AUSTRALASIA

Cities of Australasia to Be Worked.—Repeatedly during the last five years, it has been presented to me that a great work is to be done in the cities of Australasia, that the present is a favorable time to work, and that no time should be lost; and recently light has come to me, encouraging us to put forth greater efforts in Sydney, Melbourne, and Brisbane, and indicating that the time has come for us to enter Newcastle and its surrounding towns. Several small companies were presented to me, and with them two larger companies that were stretching out their hands imploringly, saying, " 'Come over . . . , and help us.' We are starving for the Bread of life."—*Review and Herald,* April 11, 1899.

Health Evangelism Work to Be Leading Edge in Australia.—The medical missionary work promises to do more in Australia than it has in America to open the way for the truth to gain access to the people. May the Lord's people now heed the invitations of God's opening providence, and realize that it is an opportune time to work.—Letter 41, 1899 (*Evangelism,* pp. 425, 426).

Health Institutions Provide Character to Work in New Fields.—At our meetings in Australia, lectures on health subjects were given daily, and a deep interest was aroused. A tent for the use of physicians and nurses was on the ground; medical advice was given freely, and was sought by many. Thousands of people attended the lectures, and at the close of the camp meeting the people were not satisfied to let the matter drop with what they had already learned. In several cities where camp meetings were held, some of the leading citizens urged that a branch sanitarium be established, promising their cooperation. In several cities the work has been started, with good success. A health institution, rightly conducted, gives character to our work in new fields. And not only is it a benefit to the people, but the workers connected with it can be a help to the laborers in evangelistic lines.

In every city where we have a church there is need of a place where treatment can be given. Among the homes of our church members there are few that afford room and facilities for the proper care of the sick. A place should be provided where treatment may be given for common ailments. The building might be inelegant and even rude, but it should be furnished with facilities for giving simple treatments. These, skillfully employed, would prove a blessing not only to our people, but to their neighbors, and might be the means of calling the attention of many to health principles.—*Testimonies for the Church,* vol. 6, pp. 112, 113. (1900)

Work to Radiate to Many Lands From Australia.—In their efforts to carry forward the work on solid lines and to enter new territory, our brethren and sisters in Australasia have made gifts and loans to the utmost of their ability. In times of great stress, the Lord has moved upon men and women both in Australasia and in America to acknowledge their stewardship by advancing means to help in establishing the institutions being built there. Those who have come to the help of the Lord in this way have been laying up treasure beside the throne of God.

Notwithstanding the dearth of means, much has been accomplished by the laborers in Australasia. Stern battles have been fought. Nothing but the miracle-working power of God has accomplished the work that has been done. We saw His power as we advanced from point to point; and we praise Him with heart and soul and voice. Oh, how we appreciated the lovingkindness of our God as He led us on step by step! . . .

Australasia is a divinely appointed center, from which the light of present truth is to radiate to many lands. There comes to us from far-off lands the cry, "Come over and help us." Some of these unentered, unenlightened fields are not too easily reached, and perhaps not so ready to receive the light, as the fields within our sight; but they must not be neglected. We are to push the triumphs of the cross. Our watchword is to be, Onward, ever onward. Our burden for the "regions beyond" can never be laid down until the whole earth shall be lightened with the glory of the Lord.—*Atlantic Union Gleaner,* June 17, 1903.

Melbourne, Australia

People Living in Australian Cities to Be Warned.—Our third Australian camp meeting was held in Armadale, a populous suburb of Melbourne, about three miles southeast from the center of the city. During the early part of the year our brethren had planned for the meeting to be held in Ballarat, a city of thirty thousand people, about ninety miles north from Melbourne. There is a faithful little church there that needed strengthening, and as the Australian Conference is in debt, it seemed desirable to hold the meeting where it would be less expensive than in Melbourne.

But the Lord has been giving me light about the work to be done in our large cities. The people in the cities are to be warned, and the message should go to them now. The time will come when we cannot work so freely in the large cities; but now, the people will listen to the message, and this is our time to work most earnestly for the people in the centers of population. Many will hear and obey, and carry the message to others.

The interest which began to be awakened by the camp meeting held two years ago in Brighton should be carried forward by a camp meeting in some part of Melbourne each year. When our brethren took these things into consideration, they decided that the meeting should be held in Melbourne, and in their search for a ground were led to locate in Armadale. The first plan was to locate the meeting at Northcote, where it would be convenient for our brethren and sisters. But the Lord hedged up the way at Northcote, and led them to a locality convenient to densely populated suburbs where the message had never been given.

During the meeting we have had abundant evidence that the Lord has been guiding both in the location and in the work of the meeting. A new field has been opened, and an encouraging field it appears to be. The people did not swarm upon the ground from curiosity, as at our first meeting in Brighton, and as at Ashfield last year. The majority came straight to the large meeting tent, where they listened intently to the word; and when [the] meeting was over, they quietly returned to their homes, or gathered in groups to ask questions or discuss what they had heard.—*Review and Herald,* January 7, 1896.

Sanitariums Needed Near Every Large City.—For a long time the Battle Creek Sanitarium was the only medical institution conducted by our people. But for many years light has been given that sanitariums should be established near every large city. Sanitariums should be established near such cities as Melbourne and Adelaide. And when opportunities come to establish the work in still other places, never are we to reach out the hand and say: No, you must not create an interest in other places, for fear that our patronage will be decreased.—Letter 233, 1905 (*Medical Ministry,* p. 326).

Sydney, Australia

Work in Cities Will Result in Many Souls Saved.—There is a work to do all over the world, and as we near the time of the end, the Lord will impress many minds to engage in this work. If you [Dr. Daniel H. Kress] are able to use your influence in setting in operation the work that needs to be done in Sydney, many souls will be saved who have never yet heard the truth. The cities are to be worked. The saving power of God is to go forth through them as a lamp that burneth.—Letter 79, 1905 (*Evangelism,* p. 425).

Experienced Managers Needed to Guide and Unify Evangelistic Efforts.—There is now a more decided work to be done in Sydney and the vicinity. All the suburbs are in a better condition to be worked than at any former period, and the advantages now presented in doing medical missionary work need more calculation and experience brought into the management of the work. . . .

There are many branches that will grow out of the plant now made in Sydney, and every line of work needs experienced managers, that part may unite with part, making a harmonious whole.—Letter 63a, 1898 (*Evangelism,* p. 425).

Why Do Sports Events Create More Excitement Than Do Promises of God?—The world is full of excitement. Men act as though they had gone mad over low, cheap, unsatisfying things. How excited have I seen them over the result of a cricket match! I have seen the streets in Sydney densely crowded for blocks and, on inquiring what was the occasion of the excitement, was told that some expert player of cricket had won the game. I felt disgusted.

Why are not the chosen of God more enthusiastic? They are striving for an immortal crown, striving for a home where there will be no need of the light of the sun or moon, or of lighted candle; for the Lord God giveth them light, and they shall reign for ever and ever. They will have a life that measures with the life of God; but the candle of the wicked shall be put out in ignominious darkness, and then shall the righteous shine forth as the sun in the kingdom of their Father.—*Special Testimonies for Ministers and Workers,* Series A, No. 5, p. 12 (*Counsels to Parents, Teachers, and Students,* pp. 343, 344). (1896)

ENGLAND

Work in England Not to Be Neglected for Other Work Elsewhere.—It seems to me that the necessity of the work in England is a very important question to us in this country. We talk about China and other countries. Let us not forget the English-speaking countries, where, if the truth were presented, many would receive and practice it.—*General Conference Bulletin,* April 22, 1901, p. 396 (*Evangelism,* p. 415).

England Greatly Neglected.—There is a great work to be done in England. The light radiating from London should beam forth in clear, distinct rays to regions beyond. God has wrought in England, but this English-speaking world has been terribly neglected. England has needed many more laborers and much more means. London has been scarcely touched. My heart is deeply moved as the situation in that great city is presented before me. . . . In the city of London alone no fewer than one hundred men should be engaged. The Lord marks the neglect of His work, and there will be a heavy account to settle by and by.

If the workers in America will impart to others of their great mercies, they will see prosperity in England. They will sympathize with the workers who are struggling with difficulties there, and will have the heart to say, not only in word but in action: "All ye are brethren" (Matthew 23:8). They will see a great work done in London, all through the cities of England, and throughout the different European countries.—*Testimonies for the Church,* vol. 6, pp. 25, 26. (1900)

London, England

A Great Work to Be Done in London.—London has been presented to me again and again as a place in which a great work is to be done, and I have tried to present this before our people. I spent two years in Europe, going over the field three times. And each time I went, I saw improvement in the work, and the last time a decided improvement was manifest. And oh, what a burning desire filled my heart to see this great field, London especially, worked as it should be. Why have not workers been sent there, men and women who could have planned for the advancement of the work? I have wondered why our people, those who are not ordained ministers, but who have a connection with God, who understand the Scriptures, do not open the Word to others. If they would engage in this work, great blessing would come to their own souls. God wants His people to work. To every man—and that means every woman, also—He has given His work, and this work each one is to perform according to his several ability.—*General Conference Bulletin,* April 22, 1901, p. 396 (*Daughters of God,* pp. 134, 135).

Army of Workers Needed to Evangelize London.—Let no one suppose that the work in London can be carried forward by one or two. This is not the right plan. While there must be those who can oversee the work, there is to be an army of workers striving to reach the different classes of people.

House-to-house work must be done. This work we have done in Australia, and we have seen the salvation of God as this work has been carried forward.—*General Conference Bulletin,* April 22, 1901, pp. 396, 397.

No Timidity; the Lord's Business Requires Haste.— There is need of zeal in the church, and wisdom to manage that zeal. You [E. J. Waggoner] have made altogether too tame work of saving souls. If you [would] see a work done in London and the surrounding cities, you must have a united, irresistible force; press the battle to the gate, and plant the standard firmly, as if you meant that the truth should triumph. The timidity, the cautious movements, have been faithless; there has been little expectation of results. . . .

The fact that things move slowly in England is no reason why the great missionary work shall move slowly to meet men's habits and customs for fear of surprising the people. They need to be much more surprised than they have hitherto been. The Lord's business requires haste; souls are perishing without a knowledge of the truth.—Letter 31, 1892 (*Manuscript Releases,* vol. 3, pp. 13, 14; *Evangelism,* pp. 414, 415).

GERMANY

Hygienic Restaurants and Sanitariums Needed.—In foreign countries many enterprises that require means must yet be begun and carried forward. The opening of hygienic restaurants, the establishment of sanitariums for the care of the sick and suffering, is just as necessary in Germany as in America. Let all do their best, making their boast in the Lord, and blessing others by their good works.—Letter 121, 1902 (*Evangelism,* p. 413).

German Émigrés Urged to Support School in Germany.—My German brethren and sisters in America, this message is given to me for you: God has His faithful ones in Germany and in all the other countries where Germans have scattered. Consider how much good you might do, how many people you might help, by selling the German edition of *Christ's Object Lessons,* doing all you can by your labor and by your means to share in the expense of establishing and carrying forward the school work in Germany.—Letter 121, 1902 (*The Publishing Ministry,* p. 367).

SCANDINAVIA

Outside Support Needed, but Local Members Are to Do Their Utmost.—I appeal especially to our brethren in

Scandinavia. Will you not take hold of the work which God has given you? Will you not labor to the utmost of your ability to relieve the embarrassed institutions in your field? Do not look on in despair, saying: "We can do nothing." Cease to talk discouragement. Take hold of the arm of Infinite Power. Remember that your brethren in other lands are uniting to give you help. Do not fail or be discouraged. The Lord will uphold His workers in Scandinavia if they will act their part in faith, in prayer, in hopefulness, doing all they can to advance His cause and hasten His coming.

Let a most earnest effort be made by our people in England to inspire their brethren in Scandinavia with faith and courage. Brethren, we must come up to the help of the Lord, to the help of the Lord against the mighty.

Remember that the nearer we approach the time of Christ's coming, the more earnestly and firmly we are to work; for we are opposed by the whole synagogue of Satan. We do not need feverish excitement, but that courage which is born of genuine faith.— *Testimonies for the Church,* vol. 6, pp. 474, 475. (1900)

Time Has Come to Enlarge the Work in Scandinavia.— There is a work to be done in Scandinavia. God is just as willing to work through Scandinavian believers as through American believers.

My brethren, bind up with the Lord God of hosts. Let Him be your fear, and let Him be your dread. The time has come for His work to be enlarged. Troublous times are before us, but if we stand together in Christian fellowship, none striving for supremacy, God will work mightily for us.— *Testimonies for the Church,* vol. 8, p. 38. (1904)

There Are More Openings Than Workers to Meet the Needs.— Sweden has as yet had but little labor, and the sound of the truth has reached but few ears; yet it is a good field, and earnest, persevering efforts should be made to extend the knowledge of the truth. Calls are coming in from Norway, Denmark, and Sweden for meetings to be held in the large cities, where a few have already been raised up. We look at these cities with pain that we have not more missionaries to send to them. The few who have received the truth in different places are left almost without help, when they should be visited often, and educated to become workers. The openings are many; but where are the laborers?

In Sweden most of our brethren are poor, and as they look at appearances it seems impossible for them to do much to sustain and extend the work. But in the early days of the cause in America similar difficulties had to be met.—*Review and Herald,* October 5, 1886.

Scandinavian Countries Are Promising Fields of Labor.—The condition of some of these churches had been presented to me in years past, with many things showing that Denmark, Norway, and Sweden were promising fields for labor. We knew that a great work lay before the missionaries in this field.—*Historical Sketches of the Foreign Missions of the Seventh-day Adventists,* p. 174. (1886)

Character of Work Judged by How It Is Presented to the Public.—In Örebro [Sweden], as well as in Copenhagen [Denmark], I am convinced that we might have had a good hearing if our brethren had secured a suitable hall to accommodate the people. But they did not expect much, and therefore did not receive much. We cannot expect people to come out to hear unpopular truth when the meetings are advertised to be held in a basement, or in a small hall that will seat only a hundred persons. The character and importance of our work are judged by the efforts made to bring it before the public. When these efforts are so limited, the impression is given that the message we present is not worthy of notice. Thus by their lack of faith our laborers sometimes make the work very hard for themselves.—*Historical Sketches of the Foreign Missions of the Seventh-day Adventists,* p. 200 (*Evangelism,* p. 422). (1886)

An Easy Religion Popular.—We are told that the people of these countries will be pleased with our discourses if we dwell on the love of Jesus. Of this they never tire, but we are in danger of losing our congregations if we dwell on the sterner questions of duty and the law of God. There is a spurious experience prevailing everywhere. Many are continually saying, "All that we have to do is to believe in Christ." They claim that faith is all we need. In its fullest sense, this is true; but they do not take it in the fullest sense. To believe in Jesus is to take Him as our redeemer and our pattern. If we abide in Him and He abides in us, we are partakers of His divine nature, and are doers of His word. The love of Jesus in the heart will lead to obedience to all His commandments. But the love that goes no farther than the lips is a delusion; it will not save any soul. Many reject the truths of the Bible, while they profess great love for Jesus; but the apostle John declares, "He that saith, I know him, and keepeth not his commandments, is a liar, and the truth is not in him." While Jesus has done all in the way of merit, we ourselves have something to do in the way of complying with the conditions. "If ye love me," said our Saviour, "keep my commandments."—*Historical Sketches of the Foreign Missions of the Seventh-day Adventists,* pp. 188, 189. (1886)

Copenhagen, Denmark

Honest-hearted Souls Despite the Secular Society Surrounding Them.—Copenhagen seems like Athens in Paul's day. The pursuit of wealth and pleasure engrosses the attention of the people. Atheism is popular. Eating and drinking, dancing and merry-making, are the subjects of thought and conversation. There are many large and beautiful churches; but the people, like some of the Athenians, are worshiping an unknown God. There is no lack of doctors of divinity, of learned preachers, but they are ignorant of Bible religion. . . .

It seems a difficult matter to awaken an interest in religious things in these large cities; and yet there are many honest souls in them who will yet accept the light and reflect its rays to others.

Copenhagen is sending missionaries to convert the heathen in far-off lands, when there are multitudes of her people who are as truly ignorant of God and His word. Men with the spirit of Paul are needed to preach Christ and Him crucified.—*Historical Sketches of the Foreign Missions of the Seventh-day Adventists,* p. 185. (1886)

THE WORK BEYOND

Millions Living in Africa and Asia Still Need to Hear the Gospel.—In Africa, in China, in India, there are thousands, yes, millions, who have not heard the message of the truth for this time. They must be warned. The islands of the sea are waiting for a knowledge of God. In these islands schools are to be established to prepare students to go to higher schools within reach, there to be educated and trained, and sent back to their island homes to give to others the light they have received.—*Testimonies for the Church,* vol. 9, p. 51. (1909)

The Whole World Has an Equal Claim With Us to God's Mercy.—The whole world is opening to the gospel. Ethiopia is stretching out her hands unto God. From Japan and China and India, from the still-darkened lands of our own continent, from every quarter of this world of ours, comes the cry of sin-stricken hearts for a knowledge of the God of love. Millions upon millions have never so much as heard of God or of His love revealed in Christ. It is their right to receive this knowledge. They have an equal claim with us in the Saviour's mercy. And it rests with us who have received the knowledge, with our children to whom we may impart it, to answer their cry.—*Education,* pp. 262, 263. (1903)

Despite the Odds and Difficulties, the World Still Must Be Warned.—There is in every city and every suburb a work to be done in presenting the last message of mercy to a fallen world. And while we are trying to work these destitute fields, the cry comes from far-off lands, "Come over and help us." These are not so easily reached, and perhaps not so ready for the harvest, as the fields within our sight, but they must not be neglected. We want to push the triumphs of the cross. Our watchword is to be, "Onward, ever onward!" Our burden for the "regions beyond" can never be laid down until the whole earth shall be lightened with the glory of the Lord.—*Australasian Union Conference Record,* January 1, 1900 (*Life Sketches of Ellen G. White,* p. 375).

Chapter 12

A
CASE STUDY

EVANGELIZING
SAN FRANCISCO AND OAKLAND

In 1872 James and Ellen White first visited California. Ellen White's concerns for the people living in San Francisco and Oakland became evident in the years that followed. In 1900 she returned to the United States from Australia. Soon after her arrival she purchased a home in northern California, which she named "Elmshaven." From then until her death in 1915, Ellen White authored many counsels on a great variety of topics, but she had a particular burden to evangelize the cities. Among the cities she wrote about were two in the Bay Area of northern California: San Francisco and Oakland. What follows is a sampling of her counsels on evangelizing those two cities.

San Francisco and Oakland have not been singled out for being any more important than other large cities around the world. Rather, the brief case study presented here is designed to illustrate Ellen White's concerns for evangelizing cities, as well as to sample her counsels for doing so in these two particular cities. Not everything she wrote about these two cities is included in this chapter, but the entries are sufficient to demonstrate the broad scope of the task and the total involvement of the church that she called for in mobilizing to evangelize a large city. The principles found in this case study may help guide all who are involved in city evangelism anywhere in the world to plan their work carefully, prayerfully, and comprehensively.

SPIRITUAL REVIVAL
OF INDIVIDUAL MEMBERS NEEDED

Genuine Conversion and Burden for Souls Needed by Church Members.—I ... met with the Oakland and San Francisco churches under the large tent in San Francisco. . . . I felt the burden of testimony and the great need of persevering personal efforts on the part of these churches to bring others to the knowledge of the truth. I had been shown that San Francisco and Oakland were missionary fields and ever would be. Their increase of numbers would be slow; but if all in these churches were living members and would do what they might do in getting the light before others, many more would be brought into the ranks and obey the truth. The present believers in the truth were not interested for the salvation of others as they should be. Inactivity and indolence in the cause of God would result in backsliding from God themselves, and by their example they would hinder others from going forward. Unselfish, persevering, active exertion would be productive of the very best results. I tried to impress upon them that which the Lord had presented before me, that He would have the truth presented to others by earnest, active laborers, not those who merely profess to believe it. They should not present the truth in words merely, but by a circumspect life, by being living representatives of the truth.

I was shown that those who compose these churches should be Bible students, studying the will of God most earnestly that they may learn to be laborers in the cause of God. They should sow the seeds of truth wherever they may be, at home, in the workshop, in the market, as well as in the meetinghouse. In order to become familiar with the Bible, they should read it carefully and prayerfully. . . .

Trusting in the blessing of God, the Christian is safe anywhere. In the city he will not be corrupted. In the counting room he will be marked for his habits of strict integrity. In the mechanic's shop every portion of his work will be done with fidelity, with an eye single to the glory of God. When this course is pursued by its individual members, a church will be successful. Prosperity will never attend these churches until the individual members shall be closely connected with God, having an unselfish interest in the salvation of their fellow men. Ministers may preach pleasing and forcible discourses, and much labor may be put forth to build up and make the church prosperous; but unless its individual members shall act their part as servants of Jesus Christ, the church will ever be in darkness and without strength. . . .

Some in these churches are in constant danger because the cares of this life and worldly thoughts so occupy the mind that they do not think upon God or heaven and the needs of their own souls. They rouse from their stupor now and then, but fall back again in deeper slumber. Unless they shall fully rouse from their slumbers, God will remove the light and blessings He has given them.—*Testimonies for the Church,* vol. 4, pp. 284-286. (1879)

Every Sin Preventing Cooperation With God to Be Put Away.—When a special effort to win souls is put forth by laborers of experience in a community where our own people live, there rests upon every believer in that field a most solemn obligation to do all in his power to clear the King's highway by putting away every sin that would hinder him from cooperating with God and with his brethren.

This has not always been fully understood. Satan has often brought in a spirit that has made it impossible for church members to discern opportunities for service. Believers have not infrequently allowed the enemy to work through them at the very time when they should have been wholly consecrated to God and the advancement of His work. Unconsciously they have wandered far from the way of righteousness. Cherishing a spirit of criticism and fault-finding, of pharisaical piety and pride, they grieve away the Spirit of God, and greatly retard the work of God's messengers.—*Review and Herald,* December 6, 1906.

Reconversion Needed Before Sharing Bible Truth With Others.—Night after night I can not sleep more than a few hours;

and often in the hours of the night I find myself sitting up in bed, praying to God in behalf of those who do not realize their spiritual condition; and then I arise and walk the room, and say, O Lord, set thy people in order, before it shall be everlastingly too late!

At times during these seasons of intercession, when the burden rests heavily, my heart is drawn out with great longing, and the tears start from my eyes, and I wring my hands before God, because I know there are souls in peril in the churches at Oakland and nearby places—souls who, in their condition of mind, know no more regarding how they stand before God than they would know had they never professed religion. . . .

We ought to long with all the heart for a thorough reconversion, that the truth may be enthroned in heart and mind, and that, by the aid of the Holy Spirit, we may be prepared to present the third angel's message before others who need it so much.—*Review and Herald,* December 13, 1906.

SEEK GOD'S GUIDANCE WHILE PLANNING

Humbly, Prayerfully Consult God From Start to Finish.—If, in this opportune time, the members of the churches will come humbly before God, putting out of their hearts all that is wrong, and consulting Him at every step, He will manifest Himself to them, and will give them courage in Him. We must be ready to use our God-given capabilities in the work of the Lord. We must be ready to speak words in season and out of season—words that will help and bless.

As the church members do their part faithfully, the Lord will lead and guide His chosen ministers, and strengthen them for their important work. In much prayer let us all unite in holding up their hands, and in drawing bright beams from the heavenly sanctuary. We are soul-hungry to see the work advancing as it should. Christ is our alpha and our omega. Only in His strength can we gain success.—*Review and Herald,* December 20, 1906.

THOROUGH BIBLE STUDY BY CHURCH MEMBERS

Bible Study Supersedes Worthless Reading.—We need to draw fresh supplies daily from the great storehouse of God's Word. This will give no time for novel reading, or for anything else that does not edify and strengthen for every good work.—*Review and Herald,* October 4, 1906 (*Sons and Daughters of God,* p. 325).

INVOLVEMENT BY ALL

Young and Old to Participate.—The most earnest efforts should be made to lead the older and younger members of our churches to take hold of the work where they are.—Manuscript 3, 1901 (*Manuscript Releases,* vol. 17, p. 47).

Ministers Reminded of Calling.—Shall we not do all in our power to advance the work in San Francisco and Oakland, and in all the other cities of California? Thousands upon thousands who live in the cities close by us need help in various ways. Let the ministers of the gospel remember that the Lord Jesus Christ said to His disciples, "Ye are the light of the world. A city that is set on an hill cannot be hid." "Ye are the salt of the earth: but if the salt have lost his savour, wherewith shall it be salted?"—Manuscript 81, 1902 (*The Kress Collection,* p. 139).

PREPARATION IMPORTANT

Preparation Crucial Before Evangelistic Work Begins.—Elder [William Ward Simpson] has had the big camp meeting tent pitched in Oakland. During the preparations he was right on hand to direct, and worked very hard to have the grounds approaching the tent as presentable as possible.—Letter 352, 1906 (*Evangelism,* p. 76).

MULTIFACETED EVANGELISM
PROGRAM COMMENDED

Different Avenues of Outreach Used.—During the past few years, the "beehive" in San Francisco has been indeed a busy one. Many lines of Christian effort have been carried forward. . . . These included visiting the sick and destitute, finding homes for orphans, and work for the unemployed; nursing the sick, and teaching the truth from house to house; the distribution of literature, and . . . classes on healthful living and the care of the sick. A school for the children has been conducted in the basement of the Laguna Street meeting house. For a time a working men's home and medical mission was maintained. On Market Street, near the city hall, there were treatment rooms, operated as a branch of the St. Helena Sanitarium. In the same locality was a health food store. Nearer the center of the city, not far from the Call building,[*] was . . . a vegetarian café, which was open six days in the week, and entirely closed on the Sabbath. Along the waterfront, ship mission work was carried on. At various times our ministers conducted meetings in large halls in the city. Thus the warning message was given by many.— *Review and Herald,* July 5, 1906 (*Welfare Ministry,* p. 112).

Maximize Effectiveness Through Expansion of Efforts.— In San Francisco a hygienic restaurant has been opened, also a food store and treatment rooms. These are doing a good work, but their influence should be greatly extended. Other restaurants similar to the one on Market Street should be opened in San Francisco and in Oakland.—*Testimonies for the Church,* vol. 7, p. 110. (1902)

VEGETARIAN RESTAURANTS

Restaurants to Teach Principles of Health.—If more . . .

---

[*] First skyscraper building in San Francisco, completed in 1898; originally home of the San Francisco *Call* newspaper.

restaurants could be carried on in San Francisco, what a blessing it would be. By the practical demonstration of how to prepare wholesome, palatable food without the use of meat, many would learn valuable lessons. They would become acquainted with health principles.—Manuscript 1, 1901 (*Manuscript Releases,* vol. 17, pp. 42, 43).

Sabbath to Be Upheld in Restaurants.—The question has been asked: "Should our restaurants be opened on the Sabbath?" My answer is: No, no! The observance of the Sabbath is our witness to God, the mark, or sign, between Him and us that we are His people. Never is this mark to be obliterated. . . .

We are to heed a "Thus saith the Lord," even though by our obedience we cause great inconvenience to those who have no respect for the Sabbath. On one hand we have man's supposed necessities; on the other, God's commands. Which have the greatest weight with us?—*Testimonies for the Church,* vol. 7, pp. 121, 122. (1902)

House-to-house Workers Needed to Accompany Public Meetings.—It is planned that Elder W. W. Simpson shall begin a series of meetings in Oakland within a very few weeks. With him should be associated a strong force of house-to-house workers. Bible readings[*] should be held in the homes of the people, and our literature should be circulated.—*Review and Herald,* October 4, 1906.

TRAINING WORKERS

Workers Trained to Do Personal Evangelism Outreach.— Elder and Mrs. [Stephen and Hetty] Haskell were conducting Bible studies [classes] in the forenoons, and in the afternoons the workers in training were going out and visiting from house to house. These

---

[*] Bible studies.

missionary visits, and the sale of many books and periodicals, opened the way for the holding of Bible readings [i.e., Bible studies]. . . .

Because of the importance of this work, I have urged that Elder Haskell and his wife, as ministers of God, shall give Bible instruction to those who will offer themselves for service. God will use humble men. He will make of every consecrated man a light-bearing Christian. Not the most eloquent in speech, not those who are the best versed in so-called theology, are always the most successful, but those who will work diligently and humbly for the Master.—*Review and Herald,* November 29, 1906 (portion in *Evangelism,* p. 470).

CREATIVE EVANGELISTIC METHODS

Creative, Innovative Evangelistic Methods Used.—The manner of Elder [Willliam Ward] Simpson's work reminds me of the efforts that were put forth in 1843 and 1844. He does not make prominent his own words, but reads much from the Bible, explaining one scripture by another. He dwells largely on the prophecies of Daniel and Revelation, and uses many illustrations and suitable figures to impress the truth. To represent the beasts of Daniel and Revelation, he has prepared lifelike images of papier-mâché.

Elder Simpson endeavors to avoid entering into controversy with opponents. He presents the Bible so clearly that it is evident that anyone who differs must do so in opposition to the Word of God.—*Review and Herald,* February 7, 1907.

Variety of Speakers Better Than Single Speaker.—In our tent meetings we must have speakers who can make a good impression on the people. The ability of one man, however intelligent this man may be, is insufficient to meet the need. A variety of talents should be brought into these meetings.—Manuscript 104, 1902 (*Evangelism,* p. 70).

Multiple Public Meetings Held Simultaneously.—Camp meetings must be multiplied. Place after place is to be entered. The interests can be divided, meetings being held in more than one place at the same time, if our men of ability are not kept hovering over the cities at the very time when they could reach many people in large tent meetings.—Manuscript 104, 1902 (*Manuscript Releases,* vol. 17, p. 52).

BIBLE TRUTH TO BE PRESENTED

Truth Presented Clearly but Simply.—Brother S [William Ward Simpson] is an intelligent evangelist. He speaks with the simplicity of a child. Never does he bring any slur into his discourses. He preaches directly from the Word, letting the Word speak to all classes. His strong arguments are the words of the Old and the New Testaments. He does not seek for words that would merely impress the people with his learning, but he endeavors to let the Word of God speak to them directly in clear, distinct utterance. If any refuse to accept the message, they must reject the Word.—Letter 326, 1906 (*Evangelism,* p. 204).

FOLLOW-UP NEEDED

House-to-house Work to Follow Public Meetings.—There is much house-to-house work to be done by faithful laborers. Our efforts are not to cease because public meetings have been discontinued for a time. So long as there are interested ones, we must give them opportunity to learn the truth. And the new converts will need to be instructed by faithful teachers of God's Word, that they may increase in a knowledge and love of the truth, and may grow to the full stature of men and women in Christ Jesus. They must now be surrounded by the influences most favorable to spiritual growth.—*Review and Herald,* February 14, 1907 (portion in *Evangelism,* p. 337).

CRITICS AND OPPONENTS EXIST

Opposition Will Occur, Even From Church Members.—
Two nights before I left my home, I was charged, during the visions of the nights, to tell the congregation that I should meet at Oakland on the Sabbath, that the wicked words coming from their lips regarding the supposed faults of God's servants who are doing the very best they can to spread the truth and to advance His work are all written in the heavenly books of record. Unless those who speak these words repent, they will at last find themselves outside the city of God. God will not allow a quarrelsome person to enter into the heavenly city.—Manuscript 95, 1906 (*Sermons and Talks,* vol. 1, pp. 375, 376).

GO FORWARD
IN FAITH

Forward in Faith, Watching, Waiting, and Praying.—
Christ said: "Say not ye, There are yet four months, and then cometh
harvest? behold, I say unto you, Lift up your eyes, and look on the
fields; for they are white already to harvest. And he that reapeth re-
ceiveth wages, and gathereth fruit unto life eternal: that both he that
soweth and he that reapeth may rejoice together. And herein is that
saying true, One soweth, and another reapeth. I sent you to reap that
whereon ye bestowed no labour; other men laboured, and ye are
entered into their labours." He knew that when the Holy Spirit
should be poured out on the disciples, the harvest of His seed-sow-
ing would be reaped. Thousands would be converted in a day.

To us, as surely as to the disciples of that time, Christ speaks
these words. Time is passing, and the Lord calls upon the workers
in all lines of His work to lift up their eyes and behold the fields all
ripe for the harvest. . . .

Our workers laboring in cities should read carefully the tenth
and eleventh chapters of Hebrews and appropriate to themselves
the instruction that this scripture contains. The eleventh chapter is
a record of the experiences of the faithful. Those who undertake to
work for God in our cities must go forward in faith, doing their
very best. As they watch and work and pray, God will hear and answer their petitions. They will obtain an experience that will be in-
valuable to them in their after work. "Faith is the substance of
things hoped for, the evidence of things not seen."—*Pacific Union
Recorder,* October 23, 1902.

Index of Biblical References

GENESIS
4:9, 10.................................99
18:25.............................12

DEUTERONOMY
15:11...........................104

2 KINGS
23:2.................................13
23:3................................14
23:20, 24.........................14

JOB
28:10................................12

PSALMS
33:13.............................12
48:1....................................9
48:2....................................9
127:1.............................143

ISAIAH
9:6....................................66
40:11............................100
42:3.............................129
58....................................69
59:14.............................36
61...................................133
61:4.............................133

JONAH
1:1, 2.............................13
3:3.....................................9
3:4...................................13

4:11.......................................9

HAGGAI
2:6, 7...........................166
2:8.....................................67

MATTHEW
4:13.............................146
4:23.............................146
5:13, 14.........................189
5:13-16............................99
5:14.........................98, 168
5:16................................87
9:35, 36.........................9, 10
10:7, 8............................58
11:5.............................101
12:20............................129
18:20............................141
23:8.............................177
24:37............................112
25:35, 36.......................100

MARK
16:15...............................15

LUKE
2:10.............................157
3:4...............................168
4:18...............................96
10:8, 9............................58
10:29..............................99
14:23............................105
19:13..............................48
21...................................89

JOHN

4:35 ....162, 163
4:35–38 195
14:15..182
15...163
15:5...105
15:12.......................................129
17:18..................................28, 29
17:20–23....................................29

ACTS

14:21...18
14:21, 22...................................18
16:9 ....172, 174, 184
17:4...19
17:17...................................19, 20
17:19, 20...................................20
17:23...21
18:3...21
18:9, 10.....................................31
19:8...23
19:9...23
28:31...24

ROMANS

13:4...85
14:7...159

1 CORINTHIANS

1:23...22
2:2, 4..22
2:3...23
6:20...102

2 CORINTHIANS

10:16 ....97, 98, 174, 184
10:17, 18...................................97
12:9...53

EPHESIANS

5:16...85
6:12...34

COLOSSIANS

4:14...58

2 TIMOTHY

2:9...24

HEBREWS

11:1...195
13:17...87

JAMES

2:5...101

2 PETER

1...107

1 JOHN

2:4...182

REVELATION

13:8...19
18:1–3 45
18:2...94
18:4...94
22:11...48

Index of Names and Topics

Abraham, had deep interest for Sodom 12
  had love for perishing souls 12
Actions, contentious, avoid 60
Actions of city workers important 60
Addictions, those with, ministries for
  133–136
  need to be helped 133, 134
Adelaide, sanitarium should be near 175
Affluent, the 104–106
Africa, millions living in, still need to
  hear gospel 183
Aged not to be assigned in cities 85
Air, foul, in cities 40, 41
All called to help the needy 101, 102
  to be reached 97–101
America, comparatively easy to
  evangelize 172
Amusements, devotion to 40
  sweep youth away 39
  worthless, resources wasted on 39
Angels of God, companionship of,
  promised 79, 80
  destroying, at work 44
  influence government leaders to
    oppose evil proposals 106
  moving upon minds of people 171
  to make impression on those in
    cities 91, 127
  to work with laborers 5, 116, 144
  we should cooperate with in saving
    humanity 30
  will fight powers of darkness when
    planting churches 149
  will go before laborers 27, 155
Antediluvian world 11
Antioch 18
  an excellent field of labor 17
  disciples first called Christians in 17
Antioch of Syria 17, 18

Appetite, indulgence of 34, 35
  perils of 34, 35
  perverted 34, 35
Appetites, intemperate in cities 43
  unnatural, continually exposed to
    temptation 41
Aquila and Priscilla's example as gospel
  workers 21
Armadale, third Australian camp meeting held in 174, 175
Ashfield, second Australian camp meeting held at 175
Asia, millions living in, still need to hear
  gospel 183
Asia Minor 18, 19
Athens 19–21
Attention, too little given to cities 25
Australia 172–177
  cities of, to be warned 174, 175
    to be evangelized 172
  comparatively easy to evangelize 172
  deep interest in health subjects
    aroused in 173
  health evangelism to be leading edge
    in 173
  institutions needed in 172
  missionary labor must be put forth
    in 167
  work to radiate to many lands from
    173, 174
Austria, to be evangelized 171
Awakening, thorough, needed among
  church members 28
Balance between medical and ministerial work needed 132, 133
Ballarat, Australia, camp meeting had
  been planned for 174
Baltimore, evangelistic work to be done
  in 161

must be worked again 152

Barnabas and Paul 18

Battle Creek, erection and enlargement of buildings in, not part of God's plan 147

expand the centers of interest in 147, 148

feelings and prejudices of some in, hindered work 126

fires allowed by God to decentralize church institutions 148, 149

too many Adventist buildings in 62, 140

too much centered in 76

work in, overemphasized 62, 145, 147, 148

workers to go forth from and take up work 146

Battle Creek Sanitarium, only Adventist medical institution for many years 175

fire 148

Battle Creek Tabernacle 156

"Beehive" in San Francisco, different avenues of outreach used in 190

Believers, new, care and instruction to be given to 149

to be thoroughly taught 149

Bible, many Europeans reject truths of while claiming love for Jesus 182

Bible studies should be held in homes 191

Bible study supersedes worthless reading 189

thorough, by church members 189

Bible truth, proclaim 87, 88

reconversion needed before sharing with others 187, 188

to be presented 193

unfold only as fast as understood 88

Bible workers, God calls upon, to consider needs of cities 108

wisely directed, needed 83

Bible-based presentations, wealthy reached through 106

Borrow funds at interest rather than stop the work 156, 157

Boston 152, 153

medical work to be done in 153, 154

money needed for work in 47

must be worked again 152

special work needed in 160

thousands in, waiting to hear truth 152, 153

Bribery abundant in cities 41

Brighton, first Australian camp meeting held at 175

Brisbane, greater effort needed in 172

Britain, Great, institutions being removed from 113

Brooklyn, to be evangelized 159, 160

vegetarian restaurant needed in 155, 156

Buffalo, money needed for work in 47

Buildings, falling to the ground 44

large, a mistake to build or purchase 61, 62

Burden for the cities 25-28, 47, 48, 109-112, 163, 185

for souls in cities, many carry no 25, 156

needed by church members 25, 26, 96, 97, 186, 187

of planting churches 140

to proclaim third angel's message 148

to regions beyond 174, 184

Café, vegetarian, San Francisco 190

California, missionary labor must be put forth in 167

not a dearth of means among our people in 156

southern 117

work needs to be done in 168, 169

California cities 167-170

Call building, first skyscraper in San Francisco 190

Calling, ministers reminded of 189

Camp meetings, Australian 174

being placed in cities where present truth not known 87

city, best possible speakers to be used at 91, 92

must be multiplied 193

pastors to attend 67, 68

restaurants for nonmembers to be operated at 122

small and in many places recommended 90, 166

Campuses, secular 107

Canada 170

Canvassers, God calls upon, to consider needs of cities 108

Capernaum, chosen by Jesus for evangelistic potential 16

Cause of God, focus energies on upbuilding 167

Caution regarding buying property in cities 164, 165

Centers, many small, needed 145

of influence, establish 49

Centralized, work is too 145-149

Centralizing large institutions not best 147, 148

Challenges of the cities 33-46

Character of Christ, demonstrating 128, 129

Character of God, revealed in Christ 70

Character of work, judged by how it is presented to public 181

to match truths we teach 60

Chattanooga, part of work at Nashville being taken to unwisely 66

Chicago 164, 165

caution regarding buying property in 164, 165

Christian help work being done in 124

localities outside, gospel to be presented in 165

medical mission opened in 109

money needed for work in 47

Swedish work in 164

talents, labor, and money to evangelize, used unwisely 143

to be worked from rural location 164

Children exposed to evils of cities 115

China, comparatively hard to evangelize 172

millions living in, still need to hear gospel 183

Christ, abased Himself to raise sinners to nobler life 71

character of, demonstrating 128, 129

example of 71

grace of, encircles the whole world 107

imitating the example of 129

inexpressible love of 71

modeled the characteristics of 76, 77

power of, will be revealed in our efforts 71, 72

present as sin-bearer 87

sensing need of 51, 52

the perfect pattern 70, 71

Christ's character, not just preaching, needed 70

earthly ministry illustrated gospel commission 15

example to be followed 141

love, impart knowledge of 141

work should be characterized by 142

method for reaching cities 58-60

mission charter 14, 15

Christ's Object Lessons, German edition of 179

Christian who trusts in the blessing of God is safe anywhere 186

Christianity, demonstration of genuine 71

evidence of sincere, needed 71

unselfish deeds strongest argument for 129

Christians can greatly impact cities 12

in both practice and profession, call to be 129

living in cities are to witness to others 96

to be salt of the earth 71

to labor earnestly in Master's service 86

Christlike energy, lack of 49

Church, needs to be well established 142

    work of 126

Church and school to be built for new congregations 143

Church leaders to assist in work of cities 51

    to be involved 51-53

    who neglect the cities held accountable by God 52

Church members, clustered together, lose sense of mission 148

    in cities, should use their talents to win souls 17, 18

        to join others in service 17, 18

    in West, to support evangelism in East 152

    need burden for souls 186, 187

    need genuine conversion 186, 187

    need to awake and be reconverted 28

    need to awake to need of establishing Christian missions 49

    need to wake up 48, 49

    new, stabilized by establishment of churches 18, 19

    opposition will occur from even 194

    should educate themselves to work for neighbors 96

    thorough awakening needed among 28

    thorough Bible study by 189

    to be awakened to urgency of work 50

    to be instructed how to work for others 86

    to benefit others 140, 141

    to learn to impart truth to others 86, 87

    unbalanced, undermine God's work 149, 150

    who congregate together called to wider service 146, 147

Church membership obligates us to work for God 63

Church planting, funds for, to be budgeted 64-67

    strategy for 149

Church schools, parents encouraged to send children to 115, 116

    to be established in cities 115

Church spirituality and growth proportionate to missionary zeal of members 69

Churches, establish as soon as possible 141

    establishment of, stabilizes new members 18, 19

    existing, to plant new churches 23, 24

    large, to assist smaller churches 141, 142

    new, increase number of available workers 143

    not to be dependent upon ministerial aid 140

    planting 140-150

    pray for God's guidance when planting 149

    to be established in every city 114, 140

    to be established inside cities 113, 114

    to be involved 126, 127

    to be organized 141, 142

    to serve those in need 126

    weakened by ministers hovering over them 144, 145

Cities, are barren and unworked fields 50, 51

    becoming like Sodom and Gomorrah 39

    burden for 47, 48

    can be greatly impacted by Christians 12

    challenges of 33-46

    great work needs to be done in 55

    little being done to warn those in 26

    little has been accomplished in 26, 27

    many will have to leave 38

must be evangelized without delay
25-27, 47, 55

neglect of 26-29, 32, 48, 49, 53, 61,
72, 92, 142, 144

not to be left in ignorance and sin
48, 49

should have been evangelized as
soon as light was received 25

soon to be closed to gospel message
48, 49

souls in, burden lacking for 25, 26

specific, work in 151-184

strong work to be opened in 26

teeming with iniquity 50

unwarned, see Unwarned cities

warn perishing in 60, 61

wickedness of 44

with a church, need health-care
facility 173

work in, not to be abandoned 112
will result in many souls saved
176

worked from outpost centers 11

working inside and outside 112-122

worldwide, full of crime 42

Cities and towns, evangelize unworked
90

City, every, work to be done in 183, 184

City, specific, wickedness not restricted
to any 44, 45

City dwellers, many, ignorant of Christ's
return 101

City environment, compounds health
problems for sick 40, 41

City evangelism, as important as missionary work in foreign countries 96, 97

becoming more difficult 34

conference leaders called to do 52,
53

funding of 63, 64

General Conference president called
to do 53

medical and ministerial work to be
united in 130, 131

negligence in 65, 66

needed 48-50, 56, 57, 84, 85, 101

Review and Herald editor called to do
53

sensational claims hinder 45, 46

training schools 82

City ministry, not advisable for elderly
or feeble 85

City missions 114, 115

as training schools for city workers
114

neglect of 49

will increase other calls for help 115

City work, youth to be trained to do
78-80

City workers, see Workers, city

Claims, sensational, hinder city evangelism 45, 46

Classes, cooking, to be conducted in
restaurants 121

on healthful living and care of sick,
conducted in San Francisco 190

social, see Social classes

Colaborers with Christ 123

Colonize, Adventists not to 25, 26, 140,
145-149

Colporteurs meeting with encouraging
success 171

Commandment-keeping people, bitterness against 154

Community ministry, involve members
in 50

Conduct, Christian, standards of 81

Conference officers, not to lay restraining hands on city work 56

Conference presidents, need to open way
for students to evangelize 51

Conferences, not to be stripped of funds
needed to plant churches 64, 65
to reserve funds for use in new fields
64, 65

Conflict between good and evil will
continue until end of time 34

Confusion regarding how to work the
cities 57, 58

Congregations, new, need church and
school to be built 143

planting new, priority given to 141-145

Contentious actions, avoid 60

Continental European countries, institutions needed in 172

Contracts, education 83

Conventions, visitors to 108, 109

Conversion, genuine, needed by church members 186, 187

Converts, in responsible positions, can witness where they are 24
    to be thoroughly grounded in truth 149
    wealthy, will help city evangelism 64

Cooking classes to be conducted in restaurants 121

Cooking schools to be established in Greater New York 158

Copenhagen, like Athens in Paul's day 182, 183
    meetings in, needed suitable meeting hall 181

Corinth 21-23
    as an example of first-century commercial-center evangelism 21
    many in, turned from idol worship 23
    Paul's plan of labor in 22, 23

Corruption 41-43

Countries, some easier to evangelize than others 171, 172

Covetousness and selfishness misrepresent the work of God 66, 67

Coworkers with Christ, a privilege to be 28
    in cities 28-30

Crime 41-43
    city, increases need to establish sanitariums in mountain regions 117, 118
    continually increasing in cities 42, 43
    epidemic of, exists everywhere 41
    increased, results from rejection of God 42
    increasing, unable to be solved by government leaders 38

Criticism, in New York churches, to be put away 158, 159
    of God's workers, refrain from 30, 62, 63, 167
    spirit of, grieving away Spirit of God and slowing work 187

Critics 149, 150, 194

Cross of Christ central to Christ's preaching 22

Cultivated intellects, not novices, needed 72

Culture, local, impacted Paul's message 20
    popular 39, 40

Daniel 79

Daniells, A. G. 52, 53, 109, 161
    called to do city evangelism 52, 53

Dearth of workers to evangelize New York City 157

Deeds, unselfish, strongest argument for Christianity 129

Degraded in society, obtain financial support from world to fund work for 110, 111

Delay, cities must be evangelized without 25-27, 50, 51, 55, 80, 168
    in evangelizing cities, Satan pleased with 28
    work made more difficult by 26, 27

Delayed and hindered, work has been 67

Denmark, calls for meetings to be held in large cities of 180, 181
    is promising field of labor 181

Denver, work to be done in despite challenges 165, 166

Dependence on God, trustful, is worker's strength 93, 94

Derbe 18

Destitute visited, in San Francisco 190

Difficulty of working cities increased by satanic agencies 34

Disciples, credited others for souls converted 16, 17
    first called Christians in Antioch 17
    to go to the people rather than wait 14, 15

Discipleship training needed for new believers 143, 149

Discouraged, God's messengers not to become 30, 31

Discretion needed in dealing with youth 81

Dishonesty and greed in cities 43

Display, extravagant, avoid 92-95
  contrary to will of God 94
  outward, will not accomplish work to be done 93

Displays, grand, not needed 92, 93

Disregard for God's requirements, world full of 115

Distressed, helping the 129

Dividing staff weakens work in both places 66

Donations to help support workers near Washington, D.C. 162

Doors also opened to opponents 49, 50

Dwellings, crowded, dark, unhealthful, in cities 40

East, large cities in, evangelistic work to be done in 151, 152, 161

Edge, leading 123-125

Educate men and women for God's service 140

Educated, the, evangelize 20, 104-106

Educating children 115

Educating students in country environment important to saving their souls 116

Education, of young workers, to be thorough 81
  scientific, important 73

Education contracts 83, 84

Educational institutions 115, 116

Effectiveness, maximize, through expansion of efforts 190

Effort, diligent personal, to be put forth 83
  lack of, has made work more difficult 151

Efforts, aggressive, needed 49, 50
  danger of adopting methods that produce minimal results 90

Efforts, decided, to be made on behalf of cities 55

Efforts, expansion of, will maximize effectiveness 190

1844 movement, cities impacted by, to be worked again 151, 152

Elderly, care for 136, 137
  need assistance 136
  or feeble, should not labor in crowded, unhealthful cities 85
  to be helped 136, 137

Elmshaven 185

Employment opportunities to be provided 103

Encouragement, duty to give workers 32
  for the work to be done 47
  workers in cities should receive 30

Energy, Christlike, lack of 49

England 177-179
  church members in, to inspire workers in Scandinavia 180
  comparatively easy to evangelize 172
  great work to be done in 177, 178
  greatly neglected 177, 178
  institutions needed in 172
  work in, not to be neglected for other work elsewhere 177

English-speaking countries, not to be forgotten over China and other countries 177
  comparatively easy to evangelize 171, 172

Enoch 11
  did not live with the wicked 11
  labored from outpost centers 11
  took some converts back to where he lived 11
  worked cities but did not dwell in them 118

Entering wedge, of mission work 114
  of gospel 123-127
  of health reform, wisely treated, will prove to be 133

Environmental pollution 40, 41

Ephesus 23

Equity, God wants work guided by 66, 67

Ethnic work to be conducted in all large cities 164

Europe, needs to be evangelized 177-179

Europeans, many, claim faith, but not in fullest sense 182
  reject truths of Bible while claiming love for Jesus 182

Evangelism, city, *see* City evangelism
  first commercial-center, Corinth an example of 21
  opposition to, as doors open 49, 50
  personal 95
    and humanitarian service to be combined 127, 128
    workers should be trained to do 191, 192
  public, in large cities 89-91
  throughout the entire world 99, 100
  to be done in every city 92

Evangelistic methods, creative, innovative, used 192, 193

Evangelistic program, multifaceted, commended 190

Evangelistic work, follow-up to, needed 90, 193

Evangelists, to work where religious issues agitate citizens 160
  train workers to be 77
  trained, professionals to become 105

Evangelize the wise and educated 20

Evangelizing the cities 55

Evidence of sincere Christianity needed 71

Evil, powerful current of, held in check by a few men 106

Example, of Christ 71
  teach by 60

Excuses for not doing city work demonstrate lack of vision 57, 58

Expansion of efforts will maximize effectiveness 190

Experienced workers to accompany youthful medical missionaries 80

Extravagance, every, should be cut out of our lives 104
  not to be seen in sanitarium buildings or furnishings 118, 119

Facilities, large, discouraged 61, 62

Fairs, provide outreach opportunities 108, 109
  visitors to 108, 109

Faith, advance in 64, 145, 169, 170
  claimed by many Europeans, but not in fullest sense 182
  experience in city evangelism strengthens 84
  go forward in, watching, waiting, praying 195
  proclaim truth in 188

False theories make the work more difficult 84

Fanaticism 150

Feeble or elderly, should not labor in crowded, unhealthful cities 85

Fields, foreign, not to be neglected 183, 184

Fields, many, to be worked 145
  new, allocate more funds to 65
    carry truth into 66, 67
    conferences to reserve use in 64, 65
    financial priority given to opening 65
    health institutions provide character to work in 173
    need to open 67, 125, 140
  still unworked 76

Finances, members with, Lord calls upon to use 64
  needed, will come as work is done 64

Financial details not the work of ministers 67, 68

Financial priority given to open new fields 65

Financial resources for reaching the cities 64

Financial support, obtain from world to fund work for most degraded in society 110, 111

First-class restaurants will result in inquiries 121

Flood, cities today are becoming like cities just before 112

Focus needed on preparing city workers 81, 82

Follow-up to evangelistic work needed 193

Food, impure, in cities 40
  superior, served in vegetarian restaurants, will result in inquiries 121

Food store, in San Francisco 190

Forbearance of God will one day be exhausted 44

Forbidding spirit of 52

Foreign fields not to be neglected 183, 184

France to be evangelized 171

Fraud abundant in cities 41

Freedom of individual action not respected 40

Friends, share with 96, 97

Funding city evangelism 63, 64

Funds, allocate more to new fields 65
  balanced, needed between current and new work 65, 66
  conferences to reserve, for use in new fields 64, 65
  for church planting to be budgeted 64-67
  jealousy over, prevents work from progressing 67
  will flow into treasuries as work is done 64

Gambling to be avoided 39

Games and horse racing to be avoided 39

Gatherings, large, Christ took advantage of opportunities provided by 108
  work wisely to obtain hearing at 108, 109

General Conference, in Takoma Park 55
  in Washington, D.C. 49
  must consider Greater New York in a different light 158

General Conference employees, not merely to preach, but to minister 79

Generosity toward others will not result in personal poverty 104

German church members in America urged to support school work in Germany 179

Germany 179
  hygienic restaurants and sanitariums needed in 179
  institutions needed in 172
  to be evangelized 171

God, accepts even limited talents 75
  consult humbly, prayerfully, from start to finish 188
  mercy of, see Mercy of God
  must seek wisdom from, when planting churches 149
  robbed when poor not helped 104
  we should partner with, to save humanity 30
  will honor those who honor Him 55
  will require an accounting for our abilities 75

God's character revealed in the life of Christ 70

God's guidance, seek while planning 188

God's mercy, see Mercy of God

God's Word, present the truths of 45, 46

God's work, neglect of 55
  to be built up 140

Good and evil, conflict between, will continue until end of time 34

Gospel, cities soon to be closed to 48, 49
  ministry of, in medical missionary work 131
  preparing cities to hear the 117
  present as clearly as possible 87
  responded to by poor 101
  sharing health evangelism opens doors for 123
  sharing with all classes, methods for needed 105

to be clearly presented in localities outside Chicago 165

to be preached in every city 104

to be proclaimed in all circumstances 16, 17

to the world, giving, is work God has committed to followers 59

work of, connected with medical missionary work 132

carried by our liberality and labors 56

worldwide proclamation of, work for lowest classes not to supersede 110

Gospel commission, illustrated by Christ's earthly ministry 15

is great missionary charter of God's kingdom 14, 15

Gospel wagon, may produce disappointing results 90

Government officials, Holy Spirit uses, to protect God's work 106

Grace of Christ, encircles whole world 107

Great Britain 113

Great work to be done 50

Greece to be evangelized 171

Greed and dishonesty in cities 43

Growth, continued, important 73

spiritual, results from active service 69, 70

Guidance, God's, seek while planning 188

Halls, rent, for public meetings 89, 90

Harmony with Christ, all are called to work in 28, 29

Haskell, Elder and Mrs. S. N. 83, 144, 155, 191

Health, imperiled by pollution 40

Health evangelism, expansion of, needed 127

opens doors for sharing gospel 123, 124

reaches distressed souls 125

to be leading edge in Australia 173

work necessary to advance God's work 125

workers to represent Christ's character 128

world open to 125

Health food store, in San Francisco 190

Health institutions provide character to work in new fields 173

Health ministry 123-139

is entering wedge of present truth 123

opens doors to gospel 123

prepares way for reception of truth 125

work to be started wherever churches are established 126

work to point sick to Christ 127, 128

Health principles, Adventist restaurants to teach 191

Health problems for sick, city life compounds 40, 41

Health reform, entering wedge of gospel 124

unwisely presented, creates prejudices 133

wisely presented, will prove an entering wedge 133

work, importance of 126

Healthful living, temperance includes all aspects of 135, 136

Heathen, in cities as well as in far-off lands 55

Heavenly agencies will touch hearts 91

Help, those who need our, all around us 70

Help work, Christian, to bless others 124

Helping people where they are 114

Helpless need assistance 136

Holidays, devotions to 40

encourage idleness 39

Holland to be evangelized 171

Holy Spirit, brings success to work 159

can do the work human agents cannot 95

communicates truth to the hearts of honest seekers 60, 61

empowers workers 76, 77

guided by 98

influence of, will touch hearts of those in cities 127

infusion of 76, 77

restraining influence of 106

uses government officials to protect God's work 106

will accomplished more than outward display 93

work in the power of 142

Holy Spirit's guidance, working under, brings results 160

Home field work is vital 48

Home fields, neglect of 49, 114

Homelike setting good for training missionary workers 82

Honest-hearted in New York need to be reached 156

Horse racing and games to be avoided 39

House-to-house efforts, to be made along with public preaching 95

House-to-house visits needed 96

House-to-house work 22, 23, 97, 98

in San Francisco 190

of equal importance with public effort 82

to be done in London 178

to be done in Washington, D.C., vicinity 162

to follow public meetings 193

House-to-house workers need to accompany public meetings 191

Human agents cannot do the work of the Holy Spirit 95

Human family is gospel ministers congregation 97, 98

Human nature, knowledge of, needed in evangelism 73

Humanity, interests of, to be built up 31

needs of, Christ came to meet 59, 60

relieving suffering 129

suffering, showing interest in, best way to reach hearts 102

understanding of, needed 73

we should partner with God in saving 30

web of, all are woven together 101

work for suffering 130

Hungry, those who are, to be fed 56

Hygienic restaurant in San Francisco 190, 191

Iconium 18

Ideas of the work too limited 57, 58

Idolatry, Paul preached against, in Athens 20, 21

Ignorance and sin, cities not to be left in 48, 49

Ignorant, many are honestly 88

Ignored, people of influence not to be 105, 106

India, comparatively hard to evangelize 172

millions living in, still need to hear gospel 183

Industries, various, establishment of 103

Inexpressible love of Christ 71

Influence, centers of, establish 49

people of, not to be ignored 105, 106

Inhabitants of the cities must be warned of judgment 26

Insanity increasing every day in cities 41

Institutions, educational 115, 116

needed in England, Australia, Continental European countries 172

to be located outside cities 113, 114

too much hovering around 147

Intellects, cultivated, needed 72

Intemperance, evils of, at work in cities 135

Interest, in suffering humanity, best way to reach hearts 102

personal, to be followed by personal labors 83

Interests, in sympathy for all 101

of all classes, united 101

of humanity, to be built up 31

Investment, undo, in select fields, condemned by God 66, 67

Islands of the sea, waiting for a knowledge of God 183

Italy to be evangelized 171

Jealousy over funds prevents work from progressing 67

Jerusalem 13, 14, 16, 17

Jesus chose Capernaum for evangelistic potential 16

mingled with people He served 15, 16

taught by example 15

the Master Teacher 15, 16

John the apostle 182

John the Baptist 168

Jonah's message not given in vain 13

Josiah persevered in efforts to cleanse Judah 13, 14

put away idolatry 14

Jubilee in sabbatical year promoted social equality 37

Judgment, God wants work guided by 66, 67

just, required from God 65, 66

sound, needed 61, 62

Judgments of God, called upon earth 29

on cities 43-46

Justice, God wants work guided by 66, 67

Kellogg J. H. 124, 126, 132, 145

Knowledge, advanced spiritual, to be a blessing to world 69

Kress, Daniel H. 109, 153, 176

Labor, systematic, benefits of 79

Labor in the cities 91

Labor unions, results of, promote difficult conditions in cities 38, 39

Laborers, consecrated, Lord calls for 26, 27

earnest, should be companies of 61

God will raise up 27

needed 25, 27, 67, 115

of varied gifts to be brought in 92

to go into cities and hold camp meetings 92

to unite their efforts with Christ, need for 74

together with God 63

unity among, always needed 29

Laguna Street meeting house, San Francisco, school for children conducted in 190

Law of God, opposition to 34

Lay members, to conduct evangelistic work in cities 113

Lay ministries, establish in cities 113

Leaders, call to 51, 52

church, to be involved in work of cities 51-53

duty of, to proclaim message 86

impact of, should not be underestimated 13, 14

in government, unable to solve problems of poverty in crime 37, 38

not awake to work to be accomplished 142

Leadership, local, needed 62, 63

Leading edge 123-125

Leading men, some, will stand with people of God in time of trouble 106

Liberty, religious, in last days, will be little respected by professing Christians 112

Lights, to be kindled in many places 99

Liquor, to be avoided 39, 135

Literature, Adventist, should be circulated 191

distributed, in San Francisco 190

free spiritual, to be provided in restaurants 122

Living conditions in cities 35, 36

Local work, decisions regarding, should be made locally 62, 63

Localities, work to be done in many 145

Loma Linda, California 43, 44

London, army of workers needed to evangelize 178

great work needed to be done in 178, 179

house-to-house work to be done in 178

needs at least 100 workers 177

London publishing house 113

Los Angeles, caution regarding buying property in 165

restaurants and treatment rooms to be established in 168

Lot, lived in Sodom but did not participate in iniquity 11, 12

Lukewarm performance an injury to the soul for whom Christ has died 96

Lukewarmness toward the cities for many years 31, 32

Luther 150

works of, rapidly circulated throughout Europe during Reformation 171

Lycaonia 18

Lystra 18

M Street Memorial Church 163

Management principles regarding evangelizing the cities 61, 62, 81

Managers, experienced, needed to guide and unify evangelistic efforts in Sydney 176

Market Street, San Francisco, treatment rooms operated in 190

Married couples to supervise young workers 80, 81

Mars' Hill 20

Means, build within 65, 66

extravagant outlay of will not accomplish work 93

to advance God's work 64

Medical and ministerial work to be united in city evangelism 130, 131

Medical evangelism preceding ministry 58, 59

Medical evangelist work, wisdom needed in 127

Medical mission maintained in San Francisco 190

Medical missionaries, helping hand of God 127

needed 80

preparing 77, 78

to reach higher classes 104, 105

Medical missionary work, connected with third angel's message 130, 131

connected with work of gospel 132

displays in, contrary to will of God 94

divine origin of 128

important to establish 155

in gospel ministry 131

is entering wedge of gospel 123-125, 127

is pioneer work of gospel 125

is right hand of gospel 125

is the ministry of Christ 15

is work of Christ 128

meets the needs of the suffering 59, 60

must be done in the cities 126

opens doors to gospel 123-125, 130

to be leading edge in Australia 173

to point sick to Christ 127, 128

See also Health evangelism; Health ministry; Health reform

Medical perspective, physicians to present gospel from 131

Medical work, not to be exalted above ministerial work 132

not to be separated from ministerial work 130

to accompany gospel ministry 130

to be done in Boston and other New England cities 153, 154

Medical workers, to engage in personal missionary work 108

Meetings, open-air, can be used 91

public, house-to-house work to follow 193

multiple to be held simultaneously 193

rent halls or other suitable place for 89, 90

training workers to include personal labor and 82, 83

small in many places, recommended 90, 91

Melbourne 174-176
    greater effort needed in 172
    people in this and other large cities,
        to be warned 174, 175
    sanitarium should be near 175
Melrose Sanitarium 153, 154
Memorial for God in every city 144, 151
Memorials to God, establish in many
        cities 145
Memphis, Tennessee, to be worked 167
Men and women, needed in various
        ministries 73, 74
    to be trained for ministry 76, 77
Men, some leading, will stand with peo-
        ple of God in time of trouble
        106
Mental culture needed 73
Mercy of God 34, 35, 42, 45, 55, 56
    whole world has equal claim to 183
Message, carry into new cities 65
    spread from continent to continent
        98
    to be given quickly 26, 27
    to be given with power 27
    to be translated so all nations can re-
        ceive truth 171
    to convert hearers 27, 28
Message of mercy, last, proclaim 107
Messages, warning, to be given to cities
        47
Messages God sent in past, no change in
        28
Messengers, God's, to be clothed in
        power 76
Methods, change, if results are small 21
Methods for sharing gospel with all
        classes needed 105
Methods of evangelism, unsuccessful 90
Mid-Atlantic U.S. cities 160-163
Midwestern U.S. cities 164-166
Minds to be influenced for Christ 107,
        108
Minister, gospel, world is the field for
        the 97
Minister to move to different field after
        new church is opened 144

Ministerial and medical work to be
        united in city evangelism 107,
        108, 130, 131
Ministers, called to evangelize cities 50,
        51
    conduct meetings in large halls in
        San Francisco 190
    hovering over churches should go to
        places still in darkness 147
    need to realize God's call to evangel-
        ize cities in California 167, 168
    not the only workers called upon to
        evangelize cities 18
    reminded of calling 189
    to befriend the poor 72
    young, to plant new congregations
        144
Ministers and physicians, qualified, both
        needed 77
Ministries, lay, establish in cities 113
    various, men and women needed in
        73, 74
Ministries for those with addictions
        133-136
Ministry, city, not advisable for elderly
        or feeble 85
    community, involve members in 50
    highest of all work 73, 74
    that God approves 70
    to substance abusers 134
    young men should not be deterred
        from entering 73, 74
Mission, city, see City mission
Mission, sense of, lost when church
        members cluster together 148
Mission charter, Christ's 14, 15
Mission fields all around 27
Mission service, character of those who
        would enter 83, 84
Mission work, to be done in all cities
        114
    ship, in San Francisco 190
Missionaries, home 97, 98
    needed in scarcely entered fields 171
    needed to work in new places 75
    self-supporting 74, 75

Missionary bands, organize 141
Missionary efforts, insufficient 82
    those who devote to worst part of
            cities, should not be forbidden
            110
Missionary spirit lacking 140
Missionary work, personal, medical
            workers to engage in 108
    true, members to have an intelligent
            knowledge of 140, 141
    wherever there is human suffering or
            need 98
Missions, city 114, 115
    essential in missionary work 81
Money, and talents, needed 63
    better spent reaching those who then
            can help reach others 143
    borrow in order to carry work for-
            ward 156
    borrowed, to be returned when
            called for 93
    invested in new buildings, greatly
            needed for city evangelism 62,
            110
    needed for work in cities 47
    not to be used for display 92, 93
    spent on luxuries and amusements
            rather relief of poor and suf-
            fering 36, 39, 45, 46
    to be used to open new fields 62, 140
Moran, F. B. 120
Mortensen, S. 164
Mothers, single, care for 136, 137
Mountain View, California, location of
            Pacific Press 49
Multiethnic work, to be conducted in
            New York City, Chicago, etc. 157
Multitudes, ignorant of God and the
            Bible 182
    neglected, Lord calls our attention to
            61
    of children deprived of parents and
            Christian home 136
    of cities, laborers needed among 25
        living in poverty 35, 36
        unwarned 107, 157

Murder, increasing every day in cities 41
Musical instruments, used in religious
            services 90
Nashville, institutions moved away from
            113
    location of Southern Publishing
            Association 49
    meetinghouses purchased and reded-
            icated in 113
    message in, to be conducted in sim-
            plicity 166
    to be made a center 66
Nature is God's physician 117
Nature's remedies, value of 77, 78
Need, every case of, to be noted 102
Needs of neglected areas to be studied 61
Needs of the great cities 56, 57
Needy, all called to help 101, 102
    sunshine of Son of Righteousness to
            be spread to 100
Neglect, of cities 25, 26, 32, 49, 50, 52,
            53, 61, 71, 72, 92, 145
    of England 177
    of far-off lands 173, 174, 183, 184
    of God's work 28, 29, 54, 149, 157-
            159
    of home fields 48, 49, 114
    of opportunities to present truth 160
    of personal work 83
    of San Francisco and Oakland 168,
            169
    of the poor 95
    of Washington, D.C. 161
    our, God is displeased with 89
Neglected, poor and suffering non-
            members in cities have been
            142
    work has been 105
Negligence in city evangelism 65, 66
Neighbor, is everyone in need 98, 99
Neighborhood, work for God in your
            own 95, 96
    work for those living in your 96
Neighborhood outreach 95-97
Neighbors, invite them to your home, then
            read and pray with them 96

New and current work, balanced funding needed between 65, 66

New England cities, medical work to be done in 153, 154

New England Sanitarium 153, 154

New Orleans, money needed for work in 47

    public effort needs to be made in 166

    to be worked 166, 167

    workers to have best interest of work at heart 166

New York City 154-160

    buildings of, will one day be destroyed by God 45, 46

    businessmen to be given the message 154

    churches, criticism and fault-finding in, to be put away 158, 159

    money needed to work in 47

    must be worked again 152

    to be worked now, utilizing various methods 157-159

Newcastle, Australia, effort needed in 172

Nineveh, not wholly given over to evil 12

North America, cities outside 171-183

North American cities 151-170

Northcote, Australia, way hedged up at 175

Northeastern U.S. cities 151-160

Norway, calls for meetings to be held in large cities of 180, 181

    is promising field of labor 181

Nurses, God calls upon, to consider needs of cities 108

    missionary, to be educated by physicians 77, 78

Nurturing workers in training 69-85

Oakland 168-170

    all sections of, need to be evangelized 168, 169

    evangelizing 185-194

    great work to be done in 169, 170

    too much centered in 76

    work to be advanced in 189

    would always be a missionary field 186

Offerings, mission, obligation to cities not met by giving 54

Officials, government, Holy Spirit uses, to protect God's work 106

    public, can enhance evangelistic possibilities 24

Old and young to participate in work 189

Open-air meetings, can be used in some places 91

    not as successful as personal witness 95

Openings, more, than workers to meet needs in Scandinavia 180, 181

Opponents, doors also opened to 49, 50

    exist 194

Opportunities, for expansion, missed 49

    of employment, to be provided 103

    to work in cities, take advantage of 48, 49

Opposition, to God's law 34

    will occur, even from church members 194

Örebro, Sweden, meetings in, needed suitable meeting hall 181

Oregon, missionary labor must be put forth in 167

Orphans, care for 136, 137

    homes found for, in San Francisco 190

    need assistance 136

    to be helped 136, 137

"Out of the cities" 117, 118

Outreach, neighborhood 95-97

Outreach efforts, denigrated frivolous young workers 81

    members with financial sources should support 64

Pacific Press, in Mountain View, California 49

Palmerston, New Zealand 149

Parents encouraged to send children to church schools 115, 116

Partners with God in saving humanity 30

Pattern, perfect 70, 71

Paul, encountered paganism in Athens 20

    had success in Corinth 23

    had to deal with those undermining God's work 150

    in Athens 19-21

    labored as self-supporting missionary 74, 75

    men with spirit of, needed to preach Christ 182, 183

    preached against idolatry in Athens 20, 21

    spent time in house-to-labor 22, 23

    taught Scripture-based truths 19

    violently opposed in Ephesus 23

Paul and Barnabas 18

Paul and Silas, preached to Thessalonians 19

Paul's message, impacted by local culture 20

Paul's plan of labor in Corinth 22, 23

Pearls, lost, in cities 50

People, come close to 95

    crowded in terraces and tenements, not God's purpose 40

    mingle with, meet their needs, invite to follow 59

    of influence, not to be ignored 105, 106

    to be reached where they are 97

Perishing in cities, warn 60, 61

Personal involvement needed 102, 103

Personal ministry, more time needed for 59

Personal work, needed in cities 161

Philadelphia 160

    money needed for work in 47

    must be worked again 152

Physical system, God's law for the 77, 78

Physicians, as gospel medical missionaries 131

    needed to battle disease in cities 72

    symbolize ministry of gospel 131

    to present message from medical perspective 131

Physicians and ministers, qualified, both needed 77

    to unite in proclaiming gospel in cities 107, 108

    to work together in city evangelism 131

Pisidia 18

Places that have an interest in the message, pastors to go to 67, 68

Planning, poor, results in unnecessary spending 62

Plans for long, extended work, not to be made 26, 27

Planting, church, strategy for 149

Planting churches, in cities 140-150

    pray for God's guidance when 149

Plants to be made in many cities 65, 66

Political strife abundant in cities 41

Pollution, environmental 40, 41

    imperils health 40

Poor, the 101-104

    cry of, reaches to heaven 104

    degradation of, in cities 37

    do not neglect 96

    every church to help 126

    exploitation of, by rich 36, 37

    God robbed when not helped 104

    gospel to be given to 105

    helped by compassionate 38

    ministers to befriend 72

    plight of, requires urgent assistance 35, 36

    pray for, and bring to Jesus 103

    respond to gospel 101

    restaurants for, to be operated at camp meetings 122

    suffering of, to be relieved 58, 59

    who can be benefited to be helped 103

    will always exist 104

Poor and rich, work for both, needed 109, 110

Portland, Maine, money needed for work in 47

to be worked 152

Portugal, to be evangelized 171

Positions of trust, people in high, should be educated in school of Christ 106

Poverty, in the cities 35, 36

   multitudes living in 36

   personal, will not come as a result of generosity toward others 104

   unable to be solved by governmental leaders 38

Poverty and the poor 34-37

Power of Christ, will be revealed in our efforts 71, 72

Powerful, the 104-106

Practice, Christians in 129

Pray for God's guidance when planting churches 149

Prayer, more needed 51, 52

   will accomplish more than outward display 93

Prayer and effort needed for cities 26

Preach the gospel is ever before the minister 97

Preaching, augmented with house-to-house efforts 95

   by itself, is not ministry 70

   public, not as effective as personal witness 95

Preparation crucial before evangelistic work begins 189

Prescott, W. W. 52, 53, 108, 109, 161

Present truth, aroused to give light of 76

   becoming more difficult to proclaim 34

   health ministry is entering wedge of 123

   must come to world 112

   to be carried to the cities 27

   to be given to every city 48, 49

Presentations, Bible-based, wealthy reached through 106

Presidents, conference, need to open way for students to evangelize 51

Priscilla and Aquila's example as gospel workers 21

Pride, spirit of, grieving away Spirit of God and slowing work 187

Priorities needed when working for lowest classes 110

Privileged to be a worker with Christ 63

Probation, close of, work to continue until 48

Profession, Christians in 129

Properties suitable for sanitariums should be considered 119

Property and power, inordinate love of 37

Property in cities, caution regarding buying 164, 165

Propriety, mission workers to act with 81

Propriety and sound sense needed 91

Protestant nations of Europe comparatively easy to evangelize 172

Providence will open way for advancement 145

Public evangelism in large cities 89-91

Public meetings, see Meetings, public

Publishing houses, establish outside cities 113

Reaping methods 86-111

Rebuke of God rests on people in Battle Creek for not working for Him in cities 156

Receiving, and not giving, forfeits blessings 63

   capacity for, increased as gifts used for Christ 63

Reconversion, needed before sharing Bible truth with others 187, 188

   needed before sharing third angel's message with others 188

Redlands, California, to be worked 168

Reform, great work of, demanded 59

Reform others by attacking wrong habits, little use to try to 97

Reform strategies for addicted individuals 134

Reformations to take place 29

Refusal to use talents eventually renders them useless 84

Regions beyond, labor in 98
to be kept in view 184

Religion that is easy is popular 182

Religious liberty, in last days, will be little respected by professing Christians 112

Resources, borrowed, to be returned when requested 93
distribute equitably 65, 66
to advance mission work in the cities, will increase 64
wasted on worthless amusements 39

Responsibilities, new, should not be added 49

Responsibility, individual, lost sight of 29
solemn, rests on the followers of Christ 86
those in positions of, needs of cities have been kept before 51

Restaurant, hygienic, in San Francisco 190, 191

Restaurant, vegetarian, in Chicago 164

Restaurant patrons should be given free spiritual literature 122

Restaurants, Adventist, Sabbath to be upheld in 191
to teach health principles 191
first-class, will result in inquiries 121
for nonmembers, to be operated at camp meetings 122
for poor, to be operated at camp meetings 122
hygienic, needed in Germany 179
not to be kept open on Sabbath 120
should be schools for healthful food preparation 121
that prepare food for education of nonmembers, to be operated at camp meetings 122
to be established in Los Angeles 168
to be established in New York City 155, 156
to be established in San Diego 168
to be established in tourist resort cities 168
vegetarian 120-122, 190, 191
to be established in cities 120
to be established in Greater New York 158
to be in cities 120
to serve as feeders for sanitariums 122
to teach principles of right living 120
workers at, to share spiritual food 121

Results, little expectation of, among workers in England 178, 179

Review and Herald, in Takoma Park 55
in Washington, D.C. 49

Review and Herald fire 148

Revival, spiritual, of individual members needed 186-188

Rich, become wealthy by oppressing others 36, 37
exploitation of poor by 36, 37
gospel to be given to 105

Rich and poor, work for both, needed 109, 110

Rich people in cities, servants of Christ should labor for 106

Rome 23, 24
metropolis of world 24
Paul witnessed as prisoner in 24

Rooms, treatment, see Treatment rooms

Russia to be evangelized 171

Sabbath, to be prominently heralded in public evangelism 89
to be upheld in Adventist restaurants 191

Sabbatical year in jubilee promoted social equality 37

Salt of earth, Christians to be 71

Salvation Army, methods not to be imitated 137-139
not to be condemned 137-139

Salvation to be offered to city inhabitants 27

Samaritan work 99, 114, 115, 126, 141, 142

San Diego, restaurants and treatment
        rooms to be established in 168
San Francisco 168-170
    all sections of, need to be evange
        lized 168, 169
    "beehive," different avenues of out-
        reach used in 190
    classes on healthful living and care of
        sick conducted in 190
    corruption, drunkenness, and rob-
        bery in 44
    destitute visited in 190
    evangelizing 185-194
    food store in 190
    great work to be done in 169, 170
    health food store in 190
    homes for orphans found in 190
    house-to-house work in 190
    hygienic restaurant in 190, 191
    Laguna Street meetinghouse, school
        for children conducted in 190
    medical mission maintained in 190
    ministers conduct meetings in large
        halls in 190
    ship mission work in 190
    sick nursed, visited in 190
    treatment rooms operated on Market
        Street in 190
    vegetarian café in 190
    work to be advanced in 189
    working men's home maintained in
        190
    would always be a missionary field
        186
Sanctified activity, spirit of 52
Sanitarium and school needed near
        New York City 154, 155
Sanitarium buildings, to demonstrate
        health principles 119
    to maintain simplicity 119
    to promote health and happiness, not
        extravagance 118, 119
Sanitarium rooms, to be comfortable 119
Sanitariums 116-120
    Eastern, great work to be done in
        125

    establish outside cities 113
    needed in Germany 179
    needed near every large city 175,
        176
    objectives for 120
    properties suitable for, should be
        considered 119
    smaller, to be planted 148, 149
    to be built outside cities 118, 119
    to be established away from cities
        113, 117-120
    to be established in country sur-
        roundings 117
    to be established in mountain
        regions 117, 118
    to reach all classes 116
    treatment rooms and vegetarian
        restaurants to serve as feeders
        to 122
Satan, at work in cities 33
    attempts to confuse plans 57
    instilling deceptive theories in
        human minds 154
    many rulers active agents of 106
    one of final efforts of, forming
        unions 38, 39
    plan of 42
    pleased thousands still in darkness 28
    pleased with delay in evangelizing
        cities 28
    prevents church members from dis-
        cerning opportunities for
        service 187
    purpose of, to attract people to cities
        112
    seeks to divert minds from truth 107
    seeks to keep talents inactive 84
    suggests cities can't be evangelized
        50
    tries to corrupt church members
        137-139
    tries to discourage workers 32
    tries to divide medical and minis -
        terial work 130, 131
    uses neglected children to influence
        those more carefully trained 116

will bring forward fables against Christ's teaching 146, 147

will multiply difficulties regarding work for cities 25, 26

working upon minds of men and women 112

would prefer a general overhauling of Adventist books over city evangelism 52

Satanic agencies, in every city 34

increase difficulty of working cities 34

increasing every day in cities 41

leading multitudes into destruction 107

to close doors now open to third angel's message 86

working of 33

Scandinavia 179-182

institutions needed in 172

more openings than workers to meet needs in 180, 181

outside support needed for 179, 180

time has come to enlarge work in 180

Scandinavian countries are promising fields of labor 181

Scandinavian workers to do their utmost to support work 179, 180

School and church to be built for new congregations 143

School and sanitarium needed near New York City 154, 155

Schools, advanced, to be established in mountain regions 117, 118

church, parents encouraged to send children to 115, 116

to be established in cities 115

instrumentality for developing workers for Christ 72

not to be established in cities 117

teaching of religion in public, to be evangelized wherever this is an issue 160

training, for city workers, city missions as 114

Schools and sanitariums, those connected with, to teach the youth evangelistic work 74

Scientific education important 73

Scientific workers, do not feel it is not necessary to become 73

Scripture, lessons from, regarding city evangelism 11-24

Sea, islands of, waiting for a knowledge of God 183

Secular campuses 107

Secular minded 107, 108

Self, to be hidden in Jesus 95

Self-denial needed 29, 140, 141

Self-enrichment through exploitation of poor forbidden by God 36, 37

Selfishness, to be eradicated 71, 72

Selfishness and covetousness, misrepresent the work of God 66, 67

Self-sacrifice, spirit of, needed 28, 49, 50, 75, 76, 140, 141

Self-supporting missionaries 74, 75

Sensationalism, to be avoided 45, 93

Sense and propriety needed 91

Separation, walls of, avoid needlessly building 60

Sermons in halls or churches not as successful as personal witness 95

Service, active, spiritual growth results from 69, 70

doors of, open everywhere 70

everyone to be engaged in 96

humanitarian, and personal evangelism to be combined 127, 128

Service and devotion, undivided, required 63

Service contract, training to be coupled with 83, 84

Setting, homelike, good for training missionary workers 82

Share with friends 96, 97

Sharp, Smith 66

Ship mission work, in San Francisco 190

Sick, need assistance 136

nursed, visited, in San Francisco 190

relieving the 129

Signs of Christ's soon return, preach
89

Silas and Paul preached to Thessalonians
19

Simpson, William Ward, during meetings, reads much from the
Bible 192
avoids controversy with
opponents 192
dwells on Daniel and Revelation
prophecies 192
uses illustrations and figures to
impress truth 192
held tent meetings in Redlands 168
lets Word of God speak directly to
people 193
on hand during preparations and
worked hard on grounds near
tent 189
preaches directly from Bible 193
preaches with simplicity 193
should have house-to-house workers
accompany 191

Sin, every, preventing cooperation with
God, to be put away 187

Sinfulness, world needs to be aroused to
the realization of its 44

Singing, to be included in religious
services 90

Slumber, deathlike, upon many ministers
and people 31, 32

Social classes, all to be reached 107
by sanitariums 116
higher in society, to be reached 104,
105
lowest, not all called to work exclusively for 109-111
priorities needed when working
for 110
work for, not to supersede
worldwide proclamation of
gospel 110

Social equality, God's regulations promote 37

Sodom 11, 12
cities have become as 115

Sodom and Gomorrah, cities becoming
like 39

Souls, account must be given for 87
honest, are seeking truth 61
in cities, burden for, needed by church
members 25, 26, 186, 187
perishing all around us 75
perishing for want of knowledge 86
precious, in cities 32
secure, by presenting Christ 95
waiting to be gathered into the fold
27
who have lost their courage, pray for
100

South Lancaster, Massachusetts 153

South, large cities in, evangelistic work
to be done in 161

Southern California cities, restaurants
and treatment rooms to be established in 168
to be worked 168

Southern Publishing Association, in
Nashville 49

Southern U.S. cities 166, 167

Spain, to be evangelized 171

Speakers, at city tent meetings 91, 92
best possible, to be used in city camp
meetings 92
to guard their words 92
variety of, better than one speaker
192

Spending for effect, needless, to be
avoided 93

Spirit, calm, steady, devoted, efforts
should be marked by 93
combative, to be put away 88
controversial, to be put away 88
of self-sacrifice needed 75, 76

Spiritual disease, evidence of 76

Spiritual food to be shared by workers
at restaurants 121

Spiritual revival of individual members
needed 186-188

Sports events create more excitement
than do promises of God 176,
177

St. Helena Sanitarium 190

St. Louis, money needed for work in 47
    1904 World's Fair in 108, 109
    to be worked 167

Staff, dividing, weakens work in both
    places 66

Stewards of God's means, all are 140, 141

Strategies, reform, for addicted individ-
    uals 134

Strategy, for church planting 149
    for reaching cities 55-68

Street education, obtained by children
    when not in school 40
    obtained by those in public schools
    115, 116

Students, called to be diligent 141
    educating in country environment
    116
    to be engaged in evangelism 51
    to labor as missionaries 80

Study, Bible, *see* Bible study

Substance abusers, ministry to 134

Success attends spirit self-denial and
    self-sacrifice 75, 76

Suicide increasing every day in cities 41

Sunday laws soon to be enforced 154

Sunday legislation, evangelists to work
    where citizens are agitated in
    minds over 160

Sweden, calls for meetings to be held in
    large cities of 180, 181
    is promising field of labor 181

Swedish Mission, Oak Street, Chicago
    164

Swedish work in Chicago 164

Sydney 176, 177
    experienced managers needed to
    guide and magnify efforts in
    176
    greater effort needed in 172

Sympathy and interest for all 101

Takoma Hall 163

Takoma Park, laborers in, to evangelize
    unworked territories 162
    location of General Conference 55
    location of Review and Herald 55
    to be worked 162
    Washington, D.C. 162, 163

Talent, special, exist to accomplish work
    56
    to be trained for work in large cities
    114

Talents, limited, God accepts even 75
    new and varied, must unite in labor
    for people 34
    refusal to use, eventually renders
    them useless 84
    variety of, needed for tent meetings
    192

Talents and influence entrusted organ-
    ized church not to be with-
    held from God's work 159

Talents and money needed 63

Teach by example 60

Teachers and helpers, lack of efficient,
    make work more difficult 84

Teaching, unbalanced 150

Teaching methods 86-111

Teaching with healing, combine 58, 59

Temperance, Christian, to be promoted
    135, 136
    includes all aspects of healthful living
    135, 136

Temperance line, work to be done
    immediately 75

Temperance ministry, youth to advance
    136

Temperance work, to be emphasized
    134, 135
    to be revived 135

Temptation, constant, weak exposed to
    in cities 41

Ten Commandments, union members
    cannot keep 38

Tenements and terraces, people crowded
    in, not God's purpose 40

Tent meetings, city, speakers at 91, 92,
    192
    to be held 137-139, 153

Territories, unentered, self-supporting
    workers needed for 74, 75

Theatergoing, stimulates passions 39

Theories, false, make the work more difficult 84

Thessalonica 19

Third angel's message, connected with medical missionary work 130, 131

medical missionary work is right hand of 125

medical workers to present 131

needed to be presented in forceful manner 56, 57

reconversion needed before sharing with others 188

restaurant workers should call attention to 121

those clustered together losing their burden to proclaim 148

those in cities to become acquainted with through labor of students 80

to be proclaimed extensively in Eastern U.S. 153

to be proclaimed in most difficult fields and most sinful cities 75, 76

to be proclaimed in northeastern U.S. cities 152

to be proclaimed with power in cities 61

to be united with second angel's message 61

unlearned and educated are to comprehend 88

Thousands, drawn by games and horse racing 39

God calls, to work for Him 123

in cities, need help 167, 168, 189

waiting to hear message 152, 153, 157, 183

may be reached with saving truth 30

need to be warned of Second Coming 142

of God-fearing men and women still in fallen churches 93, 94

still in darkness, Satan pleased that 28

to whom we can teach the truth 60

would have accepted message of truth had it been proclaimed 49

Time, end of, conflict between good and evil will continue until 34

short 61

Times, meeting the demands of the 73

Timidity, too much, among workers in England 178, 179

Topics to be preached 89

Toronto, to be evangelized 170

Tourist resort cities, restaurants and treatment rooms to be established in 168

Training, to be coupled with service contract 83, 84

Training children 115

Training schools, city evangelism 82

and public meetings, to be combined 83

for city workers, city missions as 114

Training workers 69-85, 191, 192

to include personal labor and public meetings 82, 83

Traits for effective witnessing 71, 72

Treatment rooms 122

operated in San Francisco 190

to be established in Greater New York 158

to be established in Los Angeles 168

to be established in San Diego 168

to be established in tourist resort cities 168

to serve as feeders for sanitariums 122

Treatment rooms and vegetarian restaurants to be associated together 122

Trenton, New Jersey, to be evangelized 159, 160

Truth, Bible, see Bible truth

Truth, light of, get before as many as possible 108, 109

live the 60

many people know nothing of 89

must be proclaimed throughout the world 99, 100

must be translated into different languages 171
present, see Present Truth
present as it can be grasped 88
    as it is in Jesus 49, 50, 88, 91
        at large gatherings whenever possible 108, 109
presented clearly but simply 193
proclaimers of, Christ will bless 109
sanctifying power of 159, 160
those in cities have not had presented to them 101
those who accept, to be instructed 149
thousands in Boston waiting to hear 152, 153
to be carried everywhere 98
to be presented as it is in Jesus 49, 50
to be presented in short talks 91
to be presented with power and conviction 86
unwarned multitudes must hear 107
will be presented to cities if work is done 71, 72
Truths, Scripture-based, taught by Paul 19
Turkey, to be evangelized 171
Unbalanced church members undermine God's work 149, 150
Unbelief, seeds of, sown 31, 32
    spirit of 52
Unchurched, not to be overlooked 19, 20
Unemployment, growing in cities 35, 36
Unemployment and poverty 34-37
Union members, cannot keep Ten Commandments 38
Unions 38, 39
    forming of, one of Satan's final efforts 38, 39
    workers endangered from 38
Unite work for body with work for soul 123, 124
Unity among laborers needed 29
Unreached, the 101
Unsaved, ministers to labor for 144

priority of labor to be for 144
Unwarned cities 17, 26, 47-49, 51, 52, 60, 61, 107, 108, 145, 157, 162, 163
Vegetarian café, in San Francisco 190
Vegetarian restaurants 120-122, 190, 191
    to be established in cities 120
    to serve as feeders for sanitariums 122
    to teach principles of right living 120
Vice and dissipation, habits of, acquired by children in cities 40
Vision, lack of, demonstrated through excuses for not doing city work 57, 58
Visitors to fairs and conventions 108, 109
Volunteers, needed to do evangelistic work 74
Waggoner, E. J., must have a united, irresistible force to win souls 178
Wagon, gospel, may produce disappointing results 90
Walk in harmony with our Saviour 55
Walk in the light we have been given 57
Walls of separation, avoid needlessly building 60
Warning, message of light and 5
    of destruction 12
    of judgment 13
    some must remain in cities to give last note of 112
    to be given to cities 17, 28-30, 47-49, 51-53, 60, 61, 64, 77, 95, 101, 121, 142, 154, 155, 157, 165, 174, 175, 190
    to be given to new fields 65, 146
    to be given worldwide 47, 62, 63, 75, 76, 93-95, 107, 123, 124, 134, 135, 171, 183, 184
Washington, D.C. 160-163
    evangelistic work to be done in 64, 65, 161
    few in, have been warned 160

institutions moved away from 113, 114

location of General Conference 49

location of Review and Herald 49

meetinghouses purchased and rededication 113

must be worked again 152

something must be done in, at once 160

strong evangelistic effort must be put forth in 161

workers in, not to be relocated during evangelistic meetings 161

Water, impure, in cities 40

Wealth accumulated by rich while others live in poverty 37

Wealthy, reached through Bible-based presentations 106

Wealthy converts will help city evangelism 64

Wedge, entering, see Entering wedge

Welfare of all woven together 100, 101

Wesleys 150

Western U.S. cities 167-170

Widows, need assistance 136

Willing, do not hinder 79, 80

Willis, Michigan 141

Wisdom, we must seek from God, when planting churches 149

Wise, the, evangelize 20

Witness, personal, more effective than public speaking 95

Witnessing, traits for effective 71, 72

Women and men, needed in various ministries 73, 74

to be trained for ministry 76, 77

Word of God, great truths of, will result in education of the highest order 87

unveiled truths of, to those who will listen 87

Word of truth, give to cities 65

Work, arouse and do the assigned 71, 72

character of, judged by how it is presented to public 181

to match truths we teach 60

ethnic, to be conducted in all large cities 164

for cities, far behind God's plan 25, 26

for higher classes, needs our best capabilities 105

great, needs to be done in cities 55

greatness of, to be done 50

ideas of, too limited 57, 58

in America, to be enlarged 151

in cities, not to be abandoned 112

will result in many souls saved 176

do not delay to begin 55, 56

in specific cities 151-184

local, not to be neglected 48

make no plans for long and extended 26, 27

multiethnic, to be conducted in New York City, Chicago, etc. 157

need broader view of 57, 58

new and current, balanced funding needed between 65, 66

only fraction of, has been done 115

personal, needed in cities 161

specific, God desires to be done in cities 55-57

strong, to be opened in cities 26

the cities instead of criticizing those already working there 167

to be advanced in many places 66, 67

to continue until close of probation 48

we are far behind in the 31, 32

well-balanced, to be carried on in the cities 83

young and old to participate in 189

Workers, best, to be chosen for cities 56

Bible, see Bible workers

city, actions of, important 60

focus needed on preparing 81, 82

need encouragement 30

consecrated and qualified, should be chosen for labor 79, 80 educated, essential for city work 72, 73

empowered by Holy Spirit 76, 77

endangered by unions 38

experienced, to accompany youthful medical missionaries 80

lack of experienced, a great disadvantage 61, 62

missionary, homelike setting good for training 82

needed everywhere 27
   in every city 82
   in New York City 155

nurturing in training 69-85

self-supporting, needed for unentered territories 74, 75

should be trained to do personal evangelism outreach 191, 192

to be encouraged 30-32

to be power for good 115

to evangelize New York City, dearth of 157

training 191, 192

willing, give encouragement and support to 79, 80

young, and frivolous, denigrate outreach efforts 81
   competent leaders to uphold high ideals before 79
   education of, to be thorough 81

Working men's home maintained in San Francisco 190

World, conditions in, growing worse 59
   entire, to be worked for God 99, 100
   iniquity of 115
   must still be warned 183, 184

Young and old to participate in work 189

Young people needed to work Washington, D.C., area 162

Young workers, competent leaders to uphold high ideals before 79
   education of, to be thorough 81

Youth, discretion needed in dealing with 81

God-fearing, can promote temperance 136

indulge in intemperate appetites in cities 42, 43

learned from working with experienced workers 79, 80

most able to administer to people's needs 78

swept away by amusements 39

to advance temperance ministry 136

to be blessing to society 78

to be taught to be useful adults 78

to be trained by adults of sound faith 84

to be trained to do city work 78-80

to be trained to enter new cities 79, 80

to do evangelistic work 74

to practice virtues described by apostle Peter 107

to unite their labors with older workers 79, 80

will have God's help 79